# Living in the Heart Place with Your Angels:

## Daily Angelical Whispers from Your Angels throughout the Year

## By Peg Jones

ISBN: 1482696274
ISBN 13: 9781482696271

Library of Congress Control Number: 2013904403
CreateSpace Independent Publishing Platform
North Charleston, South Carolina

# Table of Contents

# *Dedication*

I dedicate this book to my parents, who were not afraid to talk about the angels to me when I was a young child. Although as I grew older I lost interest because of life events, the basis of knowing my angels was always with me. When my interest in knowing and understanding and hearing the angels began to grow again, I remembered how special the angels truly were to me, especially when I was a young child.

I also dedicate this book to my siblings, who are a very important part of my life.

And lastly, as I save the best for the last, I dedicate this book to my best friend and husband, Jonathan, who is the true earth angel in my life. He has shown me love in so many different ways, and taught me to accept myself for who I am. He has supported me as I have pursued my hopes and dreams, and in receiving angel messages and writing this book. He has taught me to stay true to myself, as he has stayed true to me, for all the years we have been married. Thank you Jonathan for all that you have helped me with in our time of knowing each other.

# *Acknowledgements*

I would like to thank the many friends and acquaintances who encouraged me to continue writing these messages each day for the two years while I was channeling them.

Deepest thanks to T.J Phillips for encouraging me to continue with this project and your positive words when we spoke of this book. Thank you for cheering me on, and thank you for your friendship.

Thanks to Iris Weaver, Shamanic Herbalist, who has been my editor for this book. Thank you for the hours you put in editing and thank you for your friendship.

I thank the many friends on Face Book and the members of my website who have been so supportive of my channeling the angel messages. I thank each and every one of you for all that you have done in helping me to grow as I have been on my spiritual path.

# Preface

This book is my gift to you to learn about communicating with your angels. These messages have been given to you with love, from your guardian angel and other angels.

I hope that these messages are as enlightening for you as they have been for me in channeling them. My wish for you is that your days are full of love and light and that you know that your angels are with you at all times.

## Why have I written this book?

I have wanted to write a book for quite a few years. At first I thought I wanted to write about my food issues, but then I changed my mind. When I started my book in November 2009, I decided it would be about my spiritual connection and of how I came to work with the angels.

So I started by writing about my childhood, how I came to know the angels and how the angels began speaking to me as a middle-aged adult. I decided to share how the angels had helped me over the years with my confidence and my creativity and writing.

I continued to write through March 2010, when I left my job. Three weeks later, I met someone who encouraged me to begin writing messages from the angels on her podcast website and then to post the messages on Facebook and other social media websites. I was receiving positive feedback, so I continued to start each day channeling a message from my angels.

It became something I did each day.

In June 2010 I decided that I would make these messages part of my book. I felt the angels were asking me to channel a message for each day of the year, to make this into a meditation book. Once I accepted that I would make the meditations into a book, I felt the angels were asking me to include a journaling exercise for each day's message, so I added exercises for each day.

From late April till late August 2010, I channeled the messages and posted them in a blog on Blogger. At the beginning of August I lost the first three months of messages on my computer. Thank goodness for my blog! I was able to edit and use the blog to start again and put the messages month by month into a new Word document. That is when I realized the angels were really serious about me compiling these messages.

It took me from the end of April 2010 till the end of August 2012 to complete the process of channeling each message for this meditation book.

## How You Should Work With This Book

The process of reading this book will bring you through a year's journey of working and writing with your angels.

We all have angels around us. Connecting with them is a matter of inviting them to come into your life, speaking to them and then listening to their messages. Everyone is able to do this, once you understand the ways of communicating with your angels, using clairvoyance, clairaudience, clairsentience and claircognizance. It is basically using your senses of seeing, hearing, feeling and knowing. Once this is understood, communication is fairly simple.

The messages have been channeled from a group of angels and archangels. They speak of love, the heart place, healing, healing with color, how to get to your heart place, how to stop living completely in the place of the ego and many other topics.

When I was channeling these messages, there wasn't one specific way that I received the information. There were some days when I felt I needed to ask the angels a question, such as, "Do you have a message for us today?" There were other days when I felt the angels already had a specific message for me to pass along.

I think the purpose of having the messages come in different forms the way they did is so that you know that you can communicate with the angels in different ways. There is no one right way to do it. Whatever works for you is good, so within the messages you will see the different ways that I have encouraged you to communicate with the angels.

Each daily meditation has a journaling exercise pertaining in some way to the meditation. It is up to you to decide if you want use the exercise to journal or not. If you want to do the journal exercises, I suggest that you buy a journal for this purpose.

Each page has a date. There are two ways you can read this meditation book. One way is to just read each message daily, either in chronological order or as a randomly selected message. The second way is, before your day has started, read the message, go on to work and go through your day, and then before you go to bed at night, reread the message and do the journaling exercise before you go to sleep.

Throughout the book, I refer to God, Source or Higher Power. In most of my messages I use God and the pronoun Him because that is how I think. However, please don't think that you have to use that term if it doesn't work for you, nor do you have to think of him. Please know that when I use the word God I am referring to and you can use whatever term and deity/divine being you believe in--Source, Allah, Buddha, the Goddess, Great Spirit, etc.

# Living in the Heart Place with Your Angels

## January Messages

# January 1

Happy New Year to everyone. May this year be as hopeful for everyone as the last year has been. May it be a hopeful year for all. Your angels are here with you and they want to talk about what to expect in the coming year. The angels also want to talk about the possibilities of manifesting your hopes and dreams for this coming year.

## Dear Children,

We wish everyone a Happy New Year. Many of you have started new projects. They are wonderful projects and ventures. We would like to say to all of you to continue what you are doing. You will gain clarity about what you are pursuing and you will meet people who will help you along the way. The theme for this year is to help each other in all that you do.

So many people don't understand the changes that are happening throughout your planet. Those who have an inkling of what is taking place will be receiving more information to help others. We, your angels, are here for you; we are helping the changes to go smoothly. Light workers will work together and they will also work alone, but help others as they work. The Universe cares about what happens on the Earth plane and will help in any way that is asked of it.

Manifesting the hopes and dreams that are in your life will be a day-to-day experience. Be open to all whom you meet and how they may fit into your life at any particular time. What you do for others comes back to you double-fold, in many different ways. Let this be a year of self-empowerment and of manifesting all that you would like. Let the nudges and synchronicities help you to manifest all that you want. Everything is possible with the help of God and the angels. Don't be afraid to dream the impossible. Look at where you have come from and where you are going.

# January 2

## Dear Angels,

What message do you have for us today?

Be at peace, for we are here with you. Let no one overpower your free will. We ask that you stay in the heart place, with the truth and integrity that is yours. Be at peace for all is well. God and we, your angels, are with you for all time. We are here waiting for the questions which you ask from your heart. Let the Universe help you, and you can help others, too. "How can I do this?" you may ask. The answer is to just be your wonderful, giving self. All is well, because love is at the center of all.

## Journal exercise:

What questions do you have for the angels and for the Universe today? Think about it and journal about it.

# January 3

A new year is here and we will enjoy each day. Rejoice in the newness that is here. Each new step is taken to the call we hear from the Universe. Ask the angels for help and know that they will respond.

## Journal exercise:

What goals do you have for this next year? Think about it and journal about it.

# January 4

Let the good times roll, let the fun begin. A new year is upon us and we are ready to manifest good things. How your year will be is your choice. Your angels and your guides are with you. They will not interfere with your free will. They will help when you ask for help. The choices are yours, and know there is no pressure in any direction. Think about your dreams and what you would like help with. When you focus on the one thing that you want to manifest, be aware of how you are being helped and what you are doing to help it happen.

## Journal exercise:

Is there something you would like to ask the angels for help with? Think about it and journal about it.

# January 5

*Dear Angels,*

What message do you have for us today?

Thank you, dear children, for all that you do on the Earth plane to help others understand the changes that are happening at this time. We ask you to take notice of those suffering, who are in need of assistance. Your help will steer others to do what they need to do for their safety and peace of mind. Let your smile help them to know that they are loved. Let your voice assure them that all is well and that they are cared for. Finding resources for those in need is a way to help and show you care. When helping them to become self-sufficient, while knowing they are cared for, is wonderful for the helper and for those being helped. All are rewarded on a heart level. Their heart song will be heard and all will be well for everyone.

*Journal exercise:*

Is there someone you would like to help at this time? How can you help them? Think about it and journal about it.

# January 6

Let the good times roll. Each of you has a message to give and a platform from which to do this. Let your heart be the place from which you speak this message. Be at peace for your message is valid. The angels will help you know this. Never doubt the messages that are given to you, for they are given in love. Let your heart be a place of love and peace. Let your message be one for all to hear and that encourages them to come from a place of integrity. Let your truth be who you are and always be who you are. Celebrate who you are today!

## Journal exercise:

If you had to give your message to others who were waiting for your words, what would it be? Think about it and journal about it.

# January 7

Let your heart be a place where you can feel safe and peaceful at all times. Let your heart be a place where you sing your heart song. How do you want your heart place to look and to feel? You can create your own heart place and be comfortable there. Ask your angels for help with this and don't be afraid to tell them exactly what you need. When you speak to your angels in your heart place, feel the love and the clarity they send.

## Journal exercise:

Picture your heart place and how you have it designed. How does it feel? Think about it and journal about it.

# January 8

Let tranquility and peace be in your heart. Let your heart sing the joy that is there. Let the angels in and let them help you guide what is in your heart. Feel this clarity as you go through your day.

## Journal exercise:

How is your heart helping you to see all the good that there is in this world? Think about it and journal about it.

# January 9

The time is now to let the negative energy in your life be healed. It's time to clear all that is not positive. By going to your heart place, you can find the peace you are looking for. When the negative has dissipated, know that the angels have helped you with this and that they will continue to help you, if you need their help.

## Journal exercise:

What is some of the negativity you would like to have cleared? Ask the angels for their help. Think about it and journal about it.

# January 10

*Dear Angels,*

What advice do you have for us in living in the heart place?

*Dear Children,*

When living in the heart place, you know only love and peace. You know that God's love, and that of your guides and angels, is very real. When you know this, you can feel this love deep within the core of your soul. You find that life is a bit easier to live. You find the things that once bothered you no longer bother you. You feel at peace. You may find that you like being in nature. The truth of this is that the experience is different for each person who lives in the heart place. The strongest emotions are of love and of peace.

Yes, there will be times that are very tough, and you may not want to feel this love or peace. This is perfectly normal. Notice, though, that you don't lash out as much or yell as loudly as when you are not in your heart place. You may feel calmer and your reactions not be as volatile as they were in the past. When you live in the heart place, it can take time to get used to it if you have not spent time there before. Be patient with yourself and with others. Your angels will help you with this when you ask them.

*Journal exercise:*

How does it feel to spend time in your heart place? Think about it and journal about it.

# January 11

Living in the heart place is the way to consistently find joy and happiness. Being there, life feels less stressful, for you are always in the place of clarity and love. The angels remind us that the heart place has always been available to us. We just have to understand how it can be accessed, even when times are difficult.

## Journal exercise:

Have you tried to access the heart place in times when you have been off kilter? How did you get there? Think about it and journal about it.

# January 12

Your heart place is where love and the angels are. When you go there, let the peace you feel be the catalyst to show your love to all whom you know. In your heart place it is calm and there is love and peace. Know that you can be there at anytime. When you clear away the upset and the anger, love can come to the surface. The heart place will show this to you. Ask your Higher Power and your angels to help you with finding your heart place, as they are a part of it. Prayer and meditation will help bring you there, as will being with people who are in their own heart place.

## Journal exercise:

How do you know when you are in your heart place? Think about it and journal about it.

# January 13

Going to the heart place is the best way to find fulfillment and clarity in all that you do. Let your light shine brightly and let peace be felt deep in your heart. The clarity you feel will help you to know the path you are on at this time. Don't be afraid, for the angels will help you find the way to peace and to what you would like to manifest.

## Journal exercise:

What is the way to peace for you? Think about it and journal about it.

# January 14

Healing the pain is a way to help you to move on from what is negative in your life. Let the peace and love that is in your heart heal all that hurts. The healing can be physical, emotional, mental or spiritual. When you feel the love you will know that you have been healed. One way to heal the pain is to imagine using scissors to cut the cords attaching you to the person or thing causing you pain. Another way is to imagine mirrors surrounding you, with the mirrors all facing out. Doing this will help to take away the negative energy, and more peace will be felt.

## Journal exercise:

What do you do to help get rid of negative energy? Think about it and journal about it.

# January 15

Let your heart guide you to the choices that you make each day. Listen closely to the guidance given to you. Try not to be too hasty when you make your day to day decisions. Know that the guidance given to you is to help to decide if the choice is right for you. You will know if the choice is right when you feel a lot of joy and peace in your daily decision making. We, your, angels ask you to take note of the synchronicities surrounding the choice you have decided on, throughout your day.

## Journal exercise:

Did you make any choices today that came from your heart place? Think about it and journal about it.

# January 16

Come to the place that makes you happy and want to jump for joy. Bless all of you, for your hard work and attention to others and attention to detail. Be joyful, for all is well and the angels are with you, every moment of the day. Let your laughter ring out and let the joy in, deep into your heart. The day has arrived to let your dreams come true. You may only get a glimpse, or you may see the whole picture, of how your dream is coming to fruition.

## Journal exercise:

What are you seeing today for your vision? Think about it and journal about it.

# January 17

Creating the dreams in your heart means that they are heart-centered dreams. Heart-centered dreams are the best ones to have. We say this because it means the dreams are love-centered also. When you are in your love center, the love you feel in your heart spills out for others to see. This feeling of love can be contagious and instrumental in helping others to find their center. This is how the angels work, for they are always in their heart center, and help all who ask for it.

## Journal exercise:

Reach down into your heart place and ask for the guidance your angels can give to you at this time. Think about it and journal about it.

# January 18

Angel blessings are here for you. Just ask and know the blessing is for free. When you ask for help from your angels know that they are there for you anytime you dare to ask. When the angels are with you, you feel their love for you. You may feel a touch or you may feel a hug. Know that it's your angel waiting to speak to you. Let your heart be bright, and may you always find peace when you speak to your angels.

## Journal exercise:

What would you like to ask your angels for help with today? Think about it and journal about it.

# January 19

The angels' message for today is: Let the peace that is in your heart be there at all times. When the peace is present, the love is there too. When asking your angels for help with this, they will always help you be aware of their presence. Your angels will never keep you in a place that is harmful or negative. They are all about love, and how this love can be spread to all you know. It doesn't matter how many people you know. Start with one person and from there let it flow to others. For one person may know many people, who may know many other people as well. It is like a domino effect. Letting your love shine brightly to all you know will bring brightness to the world. It doesn't matter how many people see your light, just that your beacon of light has shone on those in your corner of the world and then to the rest of the world.

## Journal exercise:

How can you share your message of love from the angels to all you know? Think about it and journal about it.

# January 20

Let the newness of what you hear be a beginning. Let no one tell you how to live or to be. Begin to let the truth of who you are grow and then let it come to fruition. Let the peace in your heart always be the true test of where you are going. Let the clarity direct you in your truth. When you are clear on your path, then you travel well, and need never look back at what could have been. You look forward on your path, and see who you truly are.

## Journal exercise:

Does the peace in your heart tell you who you are, and help you to stay in your truth? Think about it and journal about it.

# January 21

As the trees move in the breeze of a sunny day, imagine angels in the trees, swaying in the breeze. The angels are dressed in many different colors, green for healing, purple for spirituality, blue for communication. One by one, they come to you and bring you beautiful gifts. You reach out for them, and you hear a song from them. You sit and listen and feel the angels' love being brought to you. You feel so blessed, and you feel so loved.

## Journal exercise:

What were the gifts given to you and what was the song that the angels sang to you? Think about it and journal about it.

# January 22

Let the possibilities of your life path be apparent to you. Let them be stepping stones to all that you want. Know that the possibilities show you what is truly in your heart. Love and peace are in your heart space. When you feel this peace and this love, know it comes from a place of clarity and of inspiration. The heart place will protect you, for the angels are there with the Source of all, whom we call God. Feel their love and be joyful at all times.

## Journal exercise:

Do you feel the angels' love? Think about it and journal about it.

# January 23

You can make the decision to move on and forgive all that has happened with a particular situation. Let this decision help you to clear the cobwebs and the fog that have blocked you from a full healing. Cutting the cords and letting go is all you can do in helping to heal. Let the Universe take care of all that is negative. Making a positive decision to move on helps to heal your heart; you may not forget, but you can forgive.

## Journal exercise:

Ask the angels to help you cut the cords of a certain issue. Think about it and journal about it.

# January 24

The heart place is where love and peace reside. Ask the angels to help you to go there today. Feel the peace and love in your heart place. Let the love of your angels take your troubles away. Let your angels help you always, for they are here for you. When you think of your heart place, think of how many angels can be in your heart place. When you have your number, know that they are there for you today, right at this moment.

## Journal exercise:

Go deep in your heart place and ask the angels to help you with whatever you would like help with. Think about it and journal about it.

# January 25

Children, we hear your voices and we hear your hopes and dreams. Think about how you want them to come to fruition and how you would like us, your angels, to help you. Go to the place in your heart where there is peace and know that you can go there at anytime. Know that we are here for you, and that we never leave you, so trust what you hear and know it is true. Thank you for all that you are, and all you are doing in this lifetime. So much has been accomplished, and you have been a big part of it.

## Journal exercise:

What dream would you like to ask your angels for help with? Think about it and journal about it.

# January 26

Embrace all that you are and all that you strive to be. It's not the lessons that have set you back. The lessons help you to grow and reach higher levels of understanding. When you understand this, then life can truly be an adventure. Forgiveness is paramount here. When you forgive, you can cope with the lessons and reasons for what happened. Let go and let the Universe bear the brunt of the pain. Ask your angels to help with this.

## Journal exercise:

What do you need to let go of today? Think about it and journal about it.

# *January 27*

## *Dear Angels*

What message do you have for today?

Today, my child, is the first day of the rest of your life. How are you going to play this day out? How are you going to be a shining light to all you meet? Will you have a busy day? Will you be happy or sad? Will you be angry or grumpy? You can choose how you react to all that is happening in your day. When things get difficult, ask God and your angels for strength. If it is a good day, thank the Universe for a wonderful day. And be grateful, no matter what your day is like. Don't lose your sense of humor, for it is a good way of coping. Open your heart and share who you are with all whom you know.

## *Journal exercise:*

How will you write about your day today? Think about it and journal about it.

# January 28

The Angel whispers that you hear today are especially for you. They are guidance from your angels to help you achieve your goals. When you hear the whispers from the angels, know they want to help and be there for you, in times of trouble and in times of great joy. The angel's whispers come from your heart place and they are always there. Sometimes you have to clear the cobwebs from the heart place so that the light shines brightly. Ask for help if you don't feel the joy that is there. Ask for clarity if something doesn't seem clear to you. The angels will help, for they care about all that is happening with you. Let your heart be filled with joy and love. Never be afraid to share your joy with others who may need to feel it. Love truly is contagious, so don't keep it to yourself but share it with others.

## Journal exercise:

What kinds of questions did you ask your angels today? How did they reply to you? Think about it and journal about it.

# January 29

Letting your heart melt into a place where kindness and peace are abundant will help you to be in a place of serenity. We, your angels, ask you to try to go to that place even when it's difficult to do so.

Ask your angels to help you go there. They can help take your doubts away. Being in the heart place brings clarity of who you are and who you want to be. Listen intently to the messages given to you, no matter how subtle they are.

## Journal exercise:

What messages are you hearing today? Think about it and journal about it.

# January 30

Creating what you want in your life takes time and patience. Letting the Universe help you with your vision will help the dream come true. Asking for help will bring the creation to reality. Sometimes the reality of co-creation is hard to comprehend. To help you to understand, every creation begins with an idea and then there is a plan to bring the idea to fruition. To understand this, think of what is already being created from your thoughts. We see this every day on the Earth plane. You are a part of this process too and sometimes that is hard to understand. We ask you to believe and trust the co-creation process.

## Journal exercise:

What do you want to co-create at this time? Think about it and journal about it.

# January 31

Never let the joy in your heart be taken away by another person. Keep joy, peace and clarity in your heart. Shine your bright light on all whom you meet. Be kind to all whom you meet and protect those who can't protect themselves.

## Journal exercise:

How can the angels help you keep feeling the joy in your heart? Think about it and journal about it.

# Living in the Heart Place with Your Angels

# February Messages

# February 1

Let fears disappear and let hope be there instead. Know that all is well when the angels are near you. Ask them for help when life is difficult and ask for guidance when life is going well. Let the peace in your heart be the one thing that is constant. When you feel this peace you will know that all is well with you in your world.

## Journal exercise:

What do you want to ask the angels for help with today? Think about it and journal about it.

# February 2

Go to the place deep within you where peace and serenity and love reside. When you get there, sit quietly and let positive energy fill your heart. Let this peace help you with your attitudes and relationships. Talking to your angels and your Higher Power will help this feeling to stay with you. Know that your angels are with you, to guide you on your path. Co-creation with the Universe will help your vision to become a reality. Never doubt how co-creation works in your world. It is a reality that will help in all you do.

## Journal exercise:

What are you co-creating with your angels and God today? Think about it and journal about it.

# February 3

*Dear Angels,*

What message do you have for us today?

*Dear Children,*

Be brave in this time of unrest in parts of the Earth plane. We are here for you. Be at peace and know that peace is the ultimate goal. Being at peace within yourself helps world peace come to fruition. We say this because peace begins within your core. Giving your pain to the Universe is a powerful way to help with healing and letting positive energy in. Ask us, your angels, for guidance with this as we are always ready to help you. Letting go of the negative is a form of self healing. Your heart will remain at peace always. Meditation helps with preserving the peace in your heart and letting your light shine brightly to all whom you meet.

*Journal exercise:*

How do you show peace of mind to others? Think about it and journal about it.

# February 4

When you are in your heart place you can rest in the feeling of peace you find there. Going to the heart place helps you to stay calm and to find clarity in any situation. To stay in the heart place you need to let go of the negative feelings and bring the positive feelings in. It is a place to rest your weary feelings and feel refreshed, and experience the love that lives there. The angels live in the heart place. When we see a rainbow, we see the beauty of the moment. When we are in our heart place, we see that all is good and serenity is at our core. Go to that place and know you are loved by all.

## Journal exercise:

What do you feel when you are in your heart place? Think about it and journal about it.

# February 5

Listen to what you are hearing in your heart today. Be at peace for all will be well. Let your worries and turmoil slip away and let your time there be rejuvenating.

## Journal exercise:

In your journal write what you are feeling and draw what you are seeing while you are in your heart place.

# February 6

*Dear Angels,*

What message do you have for us today?

When in your heart place, feel the serenity, joy and peace. Being there helps you shine your light brightly to all. Let God and the angels help you with their guidance. Let them use their love to take away your fears of asking for their help. Listen to the songs of the angels, for they are with you at all times. Give your fears to the Universe and know that divine timing works on its own schedule. You are not in control of it. As we have said many times, let divine timing and surrender make your dreams come true, for we will not leave you. Look for the signs happening around your everyday activities, letting you know the Universe is working positively to make your dreams come true. Angel Blessings to all and may your day be a day of serenity.

## Journal exercise:

How was your day today? Did you ask your angels for guidance? Think about it and journal about it.

# February 7

*Dear Angels,*

What message do you have for us today?

Today we ask you to be mindful of all that is happening in the world. We ask you to keep those who are in turmoil in the world in your prayers. Sending your love and positive energy will help to lighten the darkness in these areas. Let the peace in your heart be transmitted to those who are in pain. When you go to the heart place where peace and love are, you are helping yourself and those around you. Let peace help you to be patient and calm at each moment.

## Journal exercise:

What do you feel when you go to your heart place? Think about it and journal about it.

# February 8

*Dear Angels,*

What message do you have for us today?

Children, we would like to speak about serenity with you. When we feel serenity in our hearts we feel at peace with ourselves. We are glowing inside and out. We feel comfortable within ourselves and feel comfortable outside of ourselves; too...We have come into your lives to help you feel this way more often. With our guidance you will know that working in the heart place helps you feel peace and love and serenity. The heart place is where we shine our light brightly. Let this serenity be something that you always feel.

## Journal exercise:

What is serenity to you? Think about it and journal about it.

# February 9

## Dear Angels,

What do you have to say to us today?

Shout out your joy to all you know. Let today be joyful and bright.
Let your heart sing out with joy and let the brightness of your light
shine for all to see. Think of ways to help others to find their joy
too. Random acts of kindness are good ways to do this. Think of
all the ways you can do acts of kindness to others. Pick a different person each day for a week and see what the results are from
doing this.

## Journal exercise:

Do an act of kindness for a different person each day for a week.
Each day journal about your experience, and at the end of the
week journal about how you feel after having done this.

# February 10

## Children,

Today we come to you with our arms open wide. We want you to know that we love all that you are. We quietly watch the progress that you make each day. We see your efforts to change your planet. Know that we can help you with this. Don't be afraid to ask. Yes, we say this often, but we feel you need the reminder often.

## Journal exercise:

What would you like to ask for help with today? Think about it and journal about it.

# February 11

Children of the Earth plane:

We are here to tell you that your worries are needless. We can help when you give your worries to us. Let the Universe take care of what ails you. We work with the Universe, guiding you to solve your issues and problems. Never hesitate to ask us for help for we are always here. It seems that this is a hard concept for you to understand. Don't be afraid. Trusting us can help with your worries: by this we mean take baby steps to understand what the Universe can do for you. When trusting anyone or anything it takes time and understanding. Start out small and build up to bigger things. The trust will come.

## Journal exercise:

What small thing do you want the Universe to help you with at this time? Think about it and journal about it.

# February 12

## Children,

Imagine that you are on a cloud and you can speak to an angel of your choice. Who would this angel be and what would you talk about? When you do this exercise know that the angel you are thinking of is with you right now. You pour your heart out to them. They have a gift for you.

## Journal exercise:

What is the angel's gift and what does it mean to you? Think about it and journal about it.

# February 13

As you are dealing with the cold days of winter on this day in February, think of the warm weather that will be here in two or three months. Make an effort to get outside today. Let the breeze that you feel refresh you as you breathe in the air outside. Think of all that you are grateful for.

## Journal exercise:

Write a gratitude list in this journal. Think about it and journal about it.

# February 14

Share your love today with those who are special to you. How can you do this for each person in your life?

## Journal exercise:

Make a list of ideas of how you can show your love to the special people in your life, then choose one person and do something special for him or her.

# February 15

What are angel whispers? They are the many different messages you receive each day from your loving angels. They may be the mental nudge that keeps you from making the wrong turn or tells you to stop your car at the right time. They may be the inner voice helping you to make sense of a particular situation. Angel whispers come in different ways. Some can be loud, some can be soft. The message may be short, even just a word, or it may be long. The message can be something you hear in a song or something that a little child is saying. It may be a snippet of conversation that has meaning for you that you hear as people pass by. Sometimes it's a feeling—a sensation in your stomach, the smell of a cigar or a perfume that reminds you of someone in the past. Angel whispers stay with you and are not easily forgotten. They are never negative and are full of love. So watch out for the angel whispers that you hear or see or feel. Asking your angels for guidance is a good way to start hearing them.

## Journal exercise:

What are some of the ways you have received an angel whisper lately? Think about it and journal about it.

# February 16

When you hear a message from the angels, you are in a place of complete peace. You hear the message because your heart is open to what they are telling you. You hear their music and their words of love and peace. The message brings clarity to a situation and you know just what needs to be done. Your angels have messages of love specifically for you. They tell you of what is good and what needs to be done and when. Listen for your angels' words for you will feel so much joy and so much peace. The angels won't give you more than you can tolerate. They are gentle and they will help you make your dreams come true. All is well.

## Journal exercise:

What messages have you heard lately? Think about it and journal about it.

# February 17

Seeking the peace within helps you to find the serenity and love that are deep within your heart. When you find this peace it engulfs your whole being. You can ask the angels and your guides and masters to help you to share this peace with all whom you meet. When you feel deep peace and love you know that you have found the heart place. We pray that the love in this heart place is felt by many and that the light found there shines for others to receive. The brightness of your being shows the love that is there and you can thank your angels for helping your light to shine brightly.


## Journal exercise:

Can you find your heart place? What does it feel, look, sound like? Think about it and journal about it.

# February 18

Children, listen closely with open hearts. We want to tell you of the opportunity of transforming yourselves into loving souls. We want to tell you to search deep in your hearts. Clear out the cobwebs and find the love that has been kept there but not used to capacity. When you clear out your cobwebs, you find the love and peace that are hiding there. Once you find the love and peace, we ask that you share it with those you see each day and with whom you come into contact. Love is never old and peace is never stale, for renewal happens continually throughout the day. You start out a blank slate on some level, especially when you haven't felt love in your heart place. It is quickly filled when you let the love flow in. Hesitation comes from the ego and once the love is felt, the hesitation is gone. We are all children of God and He gave us life. His love is endless and so is your love. When you feel it you will know it. Don't be afraid to ask your angels for help. They will help you to find this love if it has been lost. They want to help and they are here for you waiting for your permission. Angel Blessings to everyone.

## Journal exercise:

How do you let your love flow and how do you feel when you let this love flow? Think about it and journal about it.

# February 19

Imagine reaching into your heart place and finding all that you need. Imagine being there and designing it in a way that is comfortable for you. What colors do you see and what kind of furniture do you see? When you have finished designing your space, sit there and see if you have a message from your angels.

## Journal exercise:

What is the message and how did you feel receiving it? Think about it and journal about it.

# February 20

Staying in the heart place helps with the clarity of who you truly are on a spiritual level. Draw a picture of how you feel when you are in your heart place, then draw one when you aren't in your heart place. Notice the colors and the difference between how you felt when you drew both pictures.

## Journal exercise:

Write about it and see what conclusions you come to when you have finished both pictures.

# February 21

There are many gifts of the heart place and they come in different sizes and shapes. There is the gift of peace and love and there is no size or limit to this gift. It is free and you can take all you want without worrying that it may run out. There is also abundance, inspiration and clarity. There are no limits, feel free to ask for more at anytime.

## Journal exercise:

How do you experience the gifts of your heart place? Think about it and journal about it.

# February 22

When you are listening to your heart and when the message is positive, it's a good way to know that your angels are around and sharing a message with you. Be joyful for all is well. They sing of the peace you feel while you are there. Know that the heart place is where the angels gather. Don't be afraid to speak to them; they will listen and show you that they are here for you.

## Journal exercise:

What message did you hear, dear child? Sit and listen. Think about it and journal about it.

# February 23

Listening to music that is relaxing and comforting can bring you to the heart place. When you are there think of who is with you and what you are doing. Let your imagination go free and make the heart place into a place of beauty.

## Journal exercise:

What does your heart place look like? Think about it and journal about it.

# February 24

Being in your heart place, where there is love and peace, is a good way to keep fear out of your mind. It keeps you calm so you can deal with the issues in your life. Letting the good in, and not paying attention to the negative thoughts, helps you to focus on what is, and not on what you may project or assume. Try this for one day. A good affirmation for this is, "I have peace and love in my heart place at all times." Watch the fear dissolve, and see the calm appear and be felt throughout your entire being.

## Journal exercise:

How did using the affirmation and feeling peace in your heart place go for you today? How did you feel? Did you feel better? Think about it and journal about it.

# February 25

*Dear Children,*

Letting go of things that don't serve you anymore is a good way to keep a positive frame of mind. Living in the heart place and keeping it bright, sprinkling it with love and peace will help you feel positive at all times. Let the negative fall by the wayside; staying in the heart place will help this to happen. Asking your angels for help with this will steer you in the right direction.

## Journal exercise:

Each heart place is different in color and design. As an experiment, try drawing your very own heart place, making it your own special place. The wonderful thing about drawing your own heart place is that it is designed differently each time you draw it. Try drawing your heart place a few days in a row. See the differences in these drawings…What do they tell you? Notice the colors. Are they vibrant and healing? Think about it and journal about the experience after you have completed five drawings.

# February 26

What message do you have for us today?

"We thank you for the work you have done in finding your heart place. You are learning to appreciate the love and peace that are there. You know you are in the heart place when you feel its loving vibration and serenity. Don't be afraid to show others your light, so that this light of good will and brightness of self can illuminate the world. Let this light help those who are not in their heart place to come into their own. There is no time schedule but know that all you speak to will be touched by this light of yours. Think of what the world would be like if we were all in our own heart places!"

## Journal exercise:

What is your heart saying to you? Think about it and journal about it.

# February 27

## Dear Children,

Let the joy in your heart be forever. Let it be a part of you always. Shine your light brightly and let the world see your beacon of light. We are so pleased that you have asked us for guidance and we are so glad to able to help you. We think that the Earth plane is starting to understand a bit more about us and what we do. We thank you for your trust and we thank you for the hope you all have for the betterment of the Earth plane. You will see good results and you won't be sorry. We wish Angel Blessings and much love and light to all on the Earth plane.

## Journal exercise:

How does this message from the angels make you feel? Do you feel joy? Do you feel sadness? Think about it and journal about it.

# February 28

*Dear Children,*

We, your angels, ask each of you to take time each day to think of what you are truly grateful for in your lives. You often forget the little things that are truly a blessing and instead get caught up in your lives and focus on what seems to be wrong. Of course, many people have had a tragic or difficult event in their lives, but it is still possible to find a positive attitude.

Sometimes finding that positive attitude is very hard. Hearing that you need to find the positive in the situation can hit you the wrong way. But if you look really hard you can find something positive. When you do this, you can find at least one thing to be grateful for. When you do this consistently, you begin to do it more automatically. Your sense of well-being comes more easily when you practice looking for the positive, and even when you feel that there is nothing to be grateful for you can find something because you look a little more deeply into your heart. Ask the angels for help with this. They will be there for you and will help you to find something positive. And then you will say, "Of course, gee, never thought of that." Angel blessings today and always.

## Journal exercise:

What will you ask your angels today? Think about it and journal about it.

# *February 29*

Singing the songs of the heart is a way to be in the heart place. How can you not feel joy when singing? When you sing out loud the negative thoughts go away and you begin to feel joy. Don't worry who hears you, it comes from the heart and maybe whoever hears you will sing along with you.

## *Journal exercise:*

What songs help you to go to your heart place? Think about it and journal about it.

# Living in the Heart Place with Your Angels

# March Messages

# March 1

Today is a new month and one day closer to our spring season.

## Dear angels,

What message of hope do you have for us today?

The winter hibernation that we experienced during the winter months because of sleet, heavy snow, freezing rain and arctic temperatures is just about over. There has been much down time for many of you and slowing down of regularly scheduled activities. We feel this has been good for all of you. Now the days are getting a little longer and the skies a bit brighter and the air a bit warmer. This is a sign that the warmer days will multiply and time outside can happen more consistently. Spending more time outside is a great way to connect with the Universe and your angels. Look for signs of spring: in the leafing of the trees, in the wakening of the flower beds and in the greening of the grass. Let go of the worries of the winter weather patterns and enjoy the soon-to-be spring weather. Let the brightness of the season be felt by all of you, and may you be as joyous as the pleasant spring days to come.

## Journal exercise:

When the season changes, do you feel a transformation within your thinking or general well-being? Think about it and journal about it.

# March 2

The angel whispers you hear are the whispers of the love that is deep in your heart space. Create this space as you would decorate a favorite room in your home, from the floor, to the ceiling, to the walls. When you have done this, sit and breathe softly, taking calm, deep breaths, and just relax. What do you hear? What do you feel? What do you know? What do you see at this time? Take it all in, and know that you have arrived at your heart place. Sit and be in the moment. Feel its warmth and its peace. As you sit there, know that your angels are there with you. Know that they have messages for you. Know that the peace and clarity you feel now can be with you always, for the heart place is where they exist. Roll back the layers of ego, and let the layers of love come in their place. Let your joy be there always, and may you share your heart place with everyone you meet.

## Journal exercise:

What does your heart space look like today? Think about it and journal about it.

# March 3

Singing the songs of the heart place is a good way to get there. Singing out in joy, singing till the sadness leaves you, is great. God says that when you sing, you are praying twice, and the joy of the song, or of the prayer, brings you right to the heart place. When we sing these songs of joy, the heart opens up and keeps reaching out for more. The heart is thirsty for song and even dance. How can you not feel joy when you are singing or dancing? Dancing in your heart place can be both calming and exciting. The movement brings you into the center of your heart place and you only feel joy. Self-expression helps to bring you joy. Of course, there are many ways of learning about the heart place. Singing and dancing are just two of the many ways you can find your way there.

## Journal exercise:

Imagine the angels dancing and singing with you in your heart space. Think about it and journal about it.

# March 4

Angel Whispers from the heart come to you most days. The angels speak of love and share love with you on the spiritual plane. They speak of how the Universe loves you dearly. They are always willing to help and yet they will not interfere with your free will. In other words, it's up to you to ask the angels for help. They will help immediately as soon as you ask for help. They will protect, encourage healing, send messages and help you to reach the vision you have for yourself. The angels won't leave you ever.

## Journal exercise:

What will you ask from the angels today? Would you like to experience a healing from them? Think about it and journal about it.

# March 5

Angel Whispers in the heart place are a way to hear the voices of the angels. They sing to you joyfully and play the songs of your heart in a pleasing way. Let their voices sing out loud, so they can be heard. When we go to the heart place, we know that we are there because of the joy we feel. How can we not feel peace, and how can we not feel joy, when we are there? Let your heart sing straight out, and know the heart place will always be there for you. It is a place without ego. It is a place where there is serenity and clarity. You don't need to fear the things that occur in the heart place because only goodness happens there.

## Journal exercise:

How is your heart place today, the same or different than it is other days? Think about it and journal about it.

# March 6

Gear up for some interesting ways of staying in your heart place. Sometimes we get to the heart place and we don't stay for long. The angels feel that if you read some ideas you will try staying in the heart place a little longer. To stay there, listen to music that is pleasing to you and have some DVDs that are pleasant to watch. There are other ways to stay in the heart place, such as writing, poetry and journaling. Being with children who are having a good time, doing a fun activity, can help you be in your heart place too.

## Journal exercise:

In your journal, write a letter to your angels or your Higher Power, then write the answer back from your angels or Higher Power.

# March 7

When we go to the heart place, there is a feeling of peace and love. We, your angels, say this to you many times so that you fully understand what this place is all about. We show you through meditation what the heart place is like and we show you through writing and song where it is. When you are there you are able to feel peace, love, clarity and joy at the same time. It's where you are centered when you are smiling and singing at the same time. We all have a heart place, but it is not felt by everyone because of different circumstances. Try to find the heart place and know that it is always within you, beneath the fog and the dark clouds. Ask your angels and God to help you with finding it. The fog will pass and the sun will shine brightly and you will feel love, peace and clarity again.

## Journal exercise:

Think about the ways your angels are helping you find your heart place. Think about it and journal about it.

# March 8

If you can stay centered in your heart place as you walk your life path, you will find peace and clarity about your life and your situation. Your life path may be rocky and hilly. There may be many bridges to cross. You may come to high places and low places as you travel your path. When you stay in the heart place on your travels, you are aware of the different conditions you encounter, yet still maintain peace and clarity. It's like the waves that come to the shoreline many times over. Some of the waves are gentle, some strong, some weak. Some waves are softer than other waves. Some waves barely touch the dry sand on the beach, while others engulf the entire beach. But no matter how small or how large the waves are, the beach is always there. Whatever the path you are traveling, you know that it's all part of the larger picture and that you survive and become enlightened. The angels want you to know that they are with you always, and that they will never leave you. So know that your angels are with you on your path and that you can speak with them. You will be aware of them through your senses at all times. Be happy, enjoy the journey, and don't forget to thank the Universe for all that comes into your life.

## Journal exercise:

Are you feeling your angels with you today? What messages are they giving to you? Think about it and journal about it.

# March 9

Imagine a time when living in the heart place is an automatic way of life. Imagine when serenity is a normal way of being at all times. Shining your light to all you meet is a good way to begin to live in the heart place. It is like a viral effect, spreading your bright light everywhere you go. Healing the heart will help this light to shine. We thank you for all you have done on the Earth plane, taking steps to reach out to others.

## Journal exercise:

How have you shone your light into the world today? Think about it and journal about it.

# March 10

Never let your fears get so big that they crush your spirit. Let the light shine deep in your heart. As you shine brightly in all that you do, know that love is the key to all happiness in your life. The angels tell us to be our best in all that we do. When we do this, we can celebrate the essence of who we truly are. Look for the signs that they are near you. Be at peace, for you are not alone.

## Journal exercise:

Have you felt your angels near you today? What words of wisdom did they have for you? Think about it and journal about it.

# March 11

Imagine a day without the guidance of your angels or God. How would it feel? Perhaps it would be like a day without inspiration. Our angels inspire so much for us, and they help us to realize our dreams, hopes and wishes. Their energy is so pleasant and they give us so much love. They truly love us and want only the best for us. The angels say, "Have no fear. Don't be afraid to ask for guidance...Don't give up hope and don't despair: we, your angels, are with you now and always....Trust and believe this. Know all things are possible."

## Journal exercise:

How have the angels helped you as you have become more familiar with them and their messages? Think about it and journal about it.

# March 12

Many angels are around us, helping us to walk on our path. We are blessed that they are so near. They help us in all the ways we ask them to. We receive their messages in many different ways. It is a joy in learning to know the different signs they share with us. When we are in the heart place we know the angels are there because that is where they live. When we understand what and where the heart place is, we know that we are safe and loved and are able to find the clarity we need. The angels are God's messengers and they have much to say to us. They guide us on our path when we ask them for help. Angel Blessings.

## Journal exercise:

How do you feel when you are in your heart place? Think about it and journal about it.

# March 13

May this day be a day of joy, and a day of vision. May your visions be of truth and integrity. May your truth bring you to where you want to be. Share the peace you feel with others when you greet them. Don't be afraid to be who you are, for the truth of you has only good intentions. Let your light shine to all you know. Know that love is all you need.

## Journal exercise:

How did you feel your joy today? Think about it and journal about it.

# March 14

Healing the heart is the key to all that is good. We can heal the heart in many different ways. We can do it through meditation, through sharing our feelings, through talking to someone who is a good listener. These are all ways of going to our heart place. We can also heal the heart through music and reading literature that helps with the healing process. We heal the heart through forgiveness and by looking at what is positive in our lives. Healing the heart can help us to move on with life's goals and to take the steps we need to reach our potential in all that we do. Healing our hearts means that we are free from what keeps us in a rut. Moving forward keeps us free in the heart place, at peace with ourselves and others.

## Journal exercise:

How do you reach your heart place, and what do you find when you get there? Think about it and journal about it.

# March 15

Today let go of your fears and feel at peace. The angels know your fears are valid, and help as much as they are able. Open your heart place a little wider to receive the angels' blessings. The angels feel it is important to remain calm despite the chaos. In continuing to hold onto hope, they ask that you help those who are in need. When you treat others as you would like to be treated, then everyone benefits. Since peace begins with the self, feeling at peace within yourself will spread to all others.

## Journal exercise:

Imagine being at peace within yourself and sharing that feeling with others. Think about it and journal about it.

# March 16

As you travel on your path in life there will be many highs and lows. Let the highs help you move along. When the lows occur take them as a time of contemplation and deep thought. Let both the high times and the low times help you grow in your life. Ask your angels to help you with your path each day and know that all is well. Each person you meet, each conversation you have, each encounter, are all a part of the path. When you understand that there are both positive and negative occurrences, then you can walk on your path a little bit easier. Listen for angel whispers and be open to what they have to say to you. Let the positive energy be abundant and find energy in your heart place. We are all beings of light and we all shine our light brightly when we are in the heart place. Let your beacon shine all around to those who need your light.

## Journal exercise:

How is your light helping others every day? Think about it and journal about it.

# March 17

What message do you have for us today?

## Dear Children,

Consider the source of the messages given to you daily. Let all the peace and clarity be from your Higher Power and the angels. Let God always be the one who is speaking clearly to you. The angels will clarify the messages and help to share them. What colors do you see in the heart place? How can you help to make the heart place a place that is safe and loving? Finding this place is sometimes difficult. But know that it is there and that you can go there at any time. What really blocks you from being there are negative feelings and emotions. Ask your angels to help you get to the heart place and feel the love, serenity and peace that are there.

## Journal exercise:

What negative emotions and feelings block you from the heart place? How can the angels help you release them? Think about it and journal about it.

# March 18

Be open to experiencing the peace and joy that are in your heart place. Know that your angels and guides are there with you. Your angels will help you keep on the path they have prepared just for you. We are all on a path to enlightenment, yet each of us has our own unique route to get there. So hold on, dear children, and enjoy the journey you are so involved with at this time. Keeping an open mind and accepting the ups and downs as they occur will bring increased understanding. Occasionally think to yourself, "What have I learned and what can I do help others as they travel on their path?"

## Journal exercise:

What really blocks us from the heart place? Think about it and journal about it.

# March 19

May your day bring you joy and enlightenment. Let the angels hear your song of woes, for they will guide you out of any negative energies that may surround you. They will help you to sing a happy tune and open your spirit to all the wonderful possibilities that exist for you. Let the day be a celebration for all to see. Be at peace, knowing your angels are with you, showing you how to feel joy at any particular time. Know that you can soar to the highest levels of joy and peace when you give your woes to your angels. Angel Blessings.

## Journal exercise:

What is bothering you today that you would like to give to your angels? Think about it and journal about it.

## March 20

Sing the song in your heart that is yearning to be sung out loud. Sing the song that is serene and full of inspiration. Let your words be positive and your intentions be true. Let the day be a day of perfection in every way. Sing the song that is true to you and is beautiful in its presentation. What are the words of your heart song today?

### Journal exercise:

Write the words for your heart song and put them together with music (you can use a tune you already know). Think about it and then write the song that is in your heart.

# March 21

*Dear Angels,*

What message do you have for us today?

We thank you for the hard work you have done and for all whom you help. We thank you for the kindnesses of each day and the gifts you give to people who are in your life. We thank you for letting others know about the angels. We hope that you understand the importance of spreading the word about the angels, so that others may know and understand about us. There are so many who have no understanding of us angels and our role in the world.

It is helpful for people to know that there are different angels who help with various aspects of their lives. There is an angel for healing, and an angel for protection and safety. There is an angel who helps with living space and an angel who helps with heavenly communication. Angels are the messengers of God. The angels also have a sense of humor and are happy when you see their humor.

*Journal exercise:*

Did the angels say something to you today that was humorous? Did it make you smile, laugh out loud? Know that they are trying to get your attention. Think about it and journal about it.

# March 22

The angels ask all who are waiting for miracles to believe that they can happen. It is important to have faith because doubt weakens the possibilities. Knowing that possibilities are endless helps you to know that miracles can happen. There is one more thing to be aware of: the angels will not in any way hurt another person or infringe on someone's free will. The miracle we want will only happen if it is for the highest good of all involved, with the best of positive intent. When these things are in place, then know your miracle can be manifested...The angels will only help when the intent is completely positive. Being positive helps manifest the miracle more readily.

## Journal exercise:

What miracle are you hoping for at this time? Think about it and journal about it.

# March 23

## Dear Children,

Letting your inner child out is a natural thing to do. It is ok to go to the safety of the heart place where pure love lives. This is where the child-like part of you lives as well. Here is where you can leave your cares behind and feel love for life as an innocent child might know it. This is where you can experience child-like play and creativity.

Healing the hurts of the inner child will help you to heal deeply. The burdens in life won't seem so overwhelming when you have healed the child within. Express what your inner child has to say to you. Your heart is a place of joy once healed, if healing is needed. Ask your angels to help you with healing your inner child. They are waiting for you now.

## Journal exercise:

Think about what your inner child feels at this time and then journal a conversation with your inner child for a few minutes.

# March 24

## Children,

Learning the lessons of life can be a difficult experience. We all learn the lessons we need to learn while on earth. Some lessons are very difficult and some are easier to learn. When we are patient with the process—and that can be difficult—everything works out for the best. Don't be afraid to let your light shine brightly for all to see.

## Journal exercise:

How do you let your light shine even when you have difficult lessons to learn? Think about it and journal about it.

# March 25

*Dear Angels,*

What is the best way to reach enlightenment today?

To reach enlightenment, do your best to live from your heart and live in a place of complete faith. This is one path to enlightenment. There are other paths too. Find what works for you, as it will take some time.

Enlightenment is when all work together to help each other understand the changes that are occurring. It is a feeling of complete satisfaction that the Universe is working in unison with you. Gathering your resources and being available to one another is part of the path of enlightenment. Know that God, your Higher Power, and your angels are helping you on your path. Live from your heart and you will find the way to enlightenment.

## Journal exercise:

What does enlightenment mean to you? Think about it and journal about it.

# March 26

## Dear Children,

Let us tell you of our love for you on the Earth plane. Sometimes we forget to tell you of this love for you. We are pure love and know nothing more than pure love...We help you to live in the heart place and to know it is a place of love. We ask you to go there and to know that all is well when you are there. It's a place where creativity and self-expression take place. Let no one take this from you. It's where you experience clarity that is free of the ego. It's where the angels and God speak to you. God does not share messages of gossip or negativity. He only shares the truth of His love and guidance for all. Be at peace and give your pain to the Universe. When you do this, you can more easily deal with the negative in your life.

## Journal exercise:

What you are hearing when you are in your heart place? Think about it and journal about it.

# March 27

## Dear Angels,

What message do you have for us today?

## Dear Children,

Please know of the importance of the changes taking place on the Earth plane. Know that we are with you at all times and that we help you when we can. Working together to help each other recover and heal makes the world a better place. Each person doing their part and each person asking for help from the Universe brings a renewed feeling of inner peace. This helps to bring peace to all as they go through their day. The Universe and the angels help you to heal. Let the peace in your heart be for you and may you have clarity about all that is occurring.

## Journal exercise:

What would you like clarity about today? Ask the angels for help with this. Think about it and journal about it.

# March 28

The signs of spring are here now. The budding of the trees, the blooming of daffodils. Watch the robins feast on worms on a rainy day. See the rabbits come out from where they hid during the winter months. Lighter jackets and clothing are being worn and children are racing around the neighborhood on their bicycles. Gardens of all kinds are being planned. Kites are being flown on windy days. What a joy it is to know that the days of winter are leaving! All is getting ready for the warmer months and soon the butterflies will be out dancing from flower to flower. The newness and the vibrancy of the coming months give us all hope and remind us of the beauty in our world. They remind us that the world is healing and the beauty this season holds is something to bring into our hearts. A metamorphosis is taking place and we are so lucky to see and feel the changes of the seasons as we live our life day to day.

## Journal exercise:

What signs of spring are you seeing at this time? Think about it and journal about it.

# March 29

*Dear Angels,*

What message do you have for us today?

Listen to the sounds around you at this moment. What sounds stand out and bring positive memories for you? Do you hear beautiful music or the songs of the birds outside? Do you hear children playing or the sounds of cars on the road? Do you hear a running brook or a dog barking in the distance? There are so many different sounds.

## *Journal exercise:*

Write down the different sounds in your world at this minute. Think about it and journal about it.

# March 30

*Dear Angels,*

What message do you have for us today?

*Children,*

Listen to your inner self when making choices for yourself. Listen only to the positive messages that come to you. When you notice negative messages, turn them around to make them more positive and empowering for you. Write down positive affirmations and keep them around your house on a card, or a mirror, or a bulletin board. Say them out loud. Each time you say them it will help you to internalize them, and tune out the negative words. Paying attention to all that is positive will help to keep you in the heart place at all times.

*Journal exercise:*

What negative message have you heard that you can turn into a positive message? Think about it and journal about it.

# March 31

Clinging to the past and not living in the present can be debilitating. The angels encourage us to live more in the present so we can make the best of each moment of our lives on the Earth plane. When we find ourselves living too much in the past, the angels ask us to practice becoming aware of each moment. What may have been very painful or abusive in the past needs to be healed. But we only have the present moment. When we truly embrace our lives moment to moment, even though we are acknowledging what is painful, we can stay positive and assure a beautiful future for ourselves.

## Journal exercise:

How have you started to live in the present? Think about it and journal about it.

# Living in the Heart Place with Your Angels

# April Messages

# April 1

Treating one another as you would like to be treated is a good philosophy to live by. You can't go wrong living this way. The peace of mind that comes when you treat everyone kindly is a sure way to know that you are living in your heart and showing your light to all you meet. Doing unto others as you would like done unto you is a way to show that you speak your truth to all. It's funny but sometimes we forget to smile or say hello to someone when we connect with strangers or with friends or family. The way we act usually influences the response we get when speaking to someone. So, when you feel a bit sad or mad or upset, make the effort to smile, to let the other person know you are happy to see them or help them, and in return you will receive the same.

## Journal exercise:

Was there a time when you experienced treating someone a certain way and they responded to you in the same way? Think about it and journal about it.

# April 2

Today we find that when we heal, we heal from the inside out. We get rid of all that is not serving our personal good. The many layers that there are will clear when we are diligent about the healing process. As these layers peel away we will start to feel better and we will be able to see and feel what living in the heart place truly is. We will feel more love and peace within ourselves than we've ever felt before. We will feel the clarity of the healing that is taking place. We will understand that we don't have to hold on to what no longer serves us. Let the Universe help you with this.

## Journal exercise:

What are you letting go of and healing today? Think about it and journal about it.

# April 3

Place your hand over your heart and let the love flow there. Just sit and imagine all the peace and love going into your heart. As you do this, ask your angels and God to help let the love flow. The angels ask you to do this because it's a way to meditate and feel calm for a few minutes. Imagine the colors of love flowing into your heart; the greens, the pinks with swirling blues and purples. As these colors swirl around your heart place, know and feel the calm and peace. This exercise is good for when you are feeling agitated or out of sorts. It will help restore the peace. It will also help you to be in a meditative state. Doing this exercise for 5-10 minutes each day will help you to have more peace and you will find living in your heart place to be a pleasant experience.

## Journal exercise:

Imagine the colors of love flowing into your heart; the greens, the pinks with swirling blues and purples. As these colors swirl around your heart place, know and feel the calmness and peace. Think about it and journal about it.

# April 4

The angels say that life is what you make of it. They say we can make it the way we desire it to be, not the way we were told it had to be. There is a big distinction between the two and it would be a real pity if we didn't understand it in our life time. When we speak to the angels they can help us see this to be true...Understanding this and making our life one of bliss can be done with baby steps. Once we get the hang of how we want to live our life, we will make progress.

## Journal exercise

Are you still bound by some of the beliefs you grew up with that may no longer serve you, or have you started to make the life you choose for yourself? How have you been able to live your truth in a way that is comfortable for you? Think about it and journal about it.

# April 5

The peace you feel in your heart lets you know you are on your path. When we dream of all that is possible for us in our lives, nothing is impossible. Think it, dream it, do it, complete it. That is all it takes. Please understand that your angels are with you and will help you with your dreams when it is for your highest good. Angel Blessings.

## Journal exercise:

What dream do you have today that you would like to manifest? How will you go about accomplishing it? Think about it and journal about it.

# April 6

*Dear Children,*

We come to you today, to say that we with you in whatever you are doing today. We want you to know that when life gets confusing or very tough we will listen to your concerns. We will guide you to think of different ways to make the situation less difficult. So tell us what is troubling you and be open to a solution from us, your angels. Go with the first thought you have and act upon it. We are here and waiting to hear from you, always.

## Journal exercise:

Have you asked for help from your angels today? Think about it and journal about it.

# April 7

Healing the pain layer by layer is a conscious decision that helps to fully heal yourself. Let the pain go layer by layer into the Universe where your angels, guides, and loved ones can handle it. The Universe takes the pain and scatters it out into space where no one can be affected by it. This helps bring you a wonderful peace and clarity that you may not have experienced before in this lifetime. The peace and love bring you right to the heart place where your angels and guides live and where God is also. Know that they are all there to help continue the healing process, forever. However painful the way, know you have heavenly support, along with your Earthly support. Appreciate both, for they are both invaluable to you.

## Journal exercise:

What have you been feeling that you would like to release to the Universe? Think about it and journal about it.

# April 8

Today, think of the ways you can bring joy to your heart even when you are in a bad mood. Ask the angels for guidance with this and tell them exactly what it is you want today. They are waiting for your request and will help you to feel the joy you are asking for. Bring your light to all you see today. Keep smiling and know that all will work out with divine timing.

## Journal exercise:

What brings joy to your heart today? Think about it and journal about it.

# April 9

When healing our pain, we open ourselves up to revisit painful memories. Letting go and giving the pain to the Universe helps to lessen it. When we live in our heart place it helps us diminish our memories of pain and focus more on happy memories. We can then see more goodness and feel more joy. It makes our hearts sing, for now we have clarity which we didn't before, understanding that pain is part of the healing process. Finally we know there is more to life than pain and we know that we can heal. The pain doesn't matter anymore because we have chosen to go beyond it. We know that our angels and guides and God help us with the healing of our hearts and souls. Feeling like no one cares is replaced with the feeling of being cared for by all in the Universe and joy is further fused into our hearts. Our hearts dance to the tune of love and serenity and we feel complete peace.

## Journal exercise:

What ways have you learned to work through the pain you have experienced in your life? Think about it and journal about it.

# April 10

## Dear Children,

Relax and know we are here. We will help you with understanding all that is possible in your lives. Let us help you with feeling peace in your heart and let us be there for you. Archangel Michael and Archangel Raphael are with you and they help you to feel safe and protected. Also know that healing is on its way. We ask you to be open to all that is happening in the Universe and to know that all is fine. We ask you to be true to yourself and to let your integrity guide you. Be at peace, let no one disturb it.

## Journal exercise:

What would you like to ask of Archangel Michael or Archangel Raphael today? Think about it and journal about it.

# April 11

*Dear Angels,*

What is your message for today?

Bringing the light into your heart helps you to see in a way that you have not seen before. It brings you to a place where love is felt at all times. It's a place that is peaceful and has only positive thoughts. The heart place will never let you down. It is where you find the daily affirmations that you write for yourself and for others in your life. The heart place is where your ego stays at the door because it is too big to enter there. When we speak of the heart place we speak of good will to everyone and we let our hearts sing out with joy. Being grateful for having what you have in your life is where healing begins. Being grateful for what is to come is a good way to stay in the heart place. We all have days that are difficult for us, so just live in the now and enjoy each moment as best as you can. We are here always and know that you can speak to us at any time.

*Journal exercise:*

Go to your heart place and see what affirmations are there for you today. Think about it and journal about it.

# April 12

Letting go of difficulties in our life is the same as letting go of stuff that we don't need. We sometimes have so much stuff (things) that we don't need in our life; we sometimes hold on to this stuff too long and it can be hard to let it go. In the same way we can have emotional stuff that holds us back. This "stuff" is what holds us down and keeps us from finding our bliss or from working in our heart place. It can be regrets, sadness, anger at yourself or others or judgments that can be harmful to yourself or to others. It is lies we believe about others and ourselves and procrastination in our everyday living. This stuff needs to be cleared and given to the Universe so that we are free of it. We can replace it with love and acceptance and integrity, peace and clarity. When we do this, there is a feeling of lightness and joy in our hearts. Our hearts beam with light and brightness and shine for all to see. The stuff is dealt with in a healing way so that we can find our true purpose without the negative getting in our way. We move on and let good fill up our hearts so that we live our true lives with minimal emotional "stuff".

## Journal exercise:

What stuff, emotional or physical, do you need to get rid of today? Think about it and journal about it.

# April 13

*Dear Children,*

We are here with you today to see if you are ready to move forward on your life path. Are you willing to take chances and to take on greater challenges? We feel you can do this if you have trust and clarity about what you need to do. We ask you to go deep within your heart and to take an inventory of what your next step will be. Letting go of fears and doubts will help you with this.

## Journal exercise:

What is next on your path? What will you do to get there? Who will help you? Think about it and journal about it.

# April 14

*Dear Angels,*

What message do you have for us today?

Let springtime be a time of new beginnings. When we think of this time of the year, we feel lighter. This is the time when days are getting longer and warmer. We see how Nature is growing and changing on a daily basis. Enjoy this time, be outside and go for long walks.

## Journal exercise:

What does the springtime mean to you and how do you celebrate its renewal? Think about it and journal about it.

# April 15

The angels ask if you sometimes sit and watch the trees swaying on windy days. The trees seem to sway to their own beat and to their own song. They have a flowing quality. Can you move to the movements of the trees with the help of some upbeat music? Trees have their own personalities and ways of communicating. They speak to us through their movements, through their shapes and forms and through the fruits they bear. They thrive when the right care is given to them. They are like humans in that they need love, nurturing, light and water to survive. We too are productive when the right care is given.

## Journal exercise:

How can you take care of yourself so that your life is productive and plentiful? Think about it and journal about it.

# April 16

Pink and white are the special colors of the heart. They are the colors of love and purity, the essence of the heart and soul. When these colors mingle together, it's like a dish of raspberry swirl ice cream. Let the two colors mix till they are one and the color represents pure, delicious love. Letting the pureness of a raspberry pinkish color be inside your heart will melt the things that don't belong there, such as anger, sadness and jealousy, as well as all the other things that don't serve us. Love is pure and has many aspects. We know what they are. Let them in slowly and ask the angels to help you with this.

## Journal exercise:

What are some of the aspects of love that you know? Think about it and journal about it.

# April 17

Tuning into your angels will help you to hear their messages. The angels speak to you in so many ways. They speak through other people and through words and sentences you read or hear each day. They speak through songs and they speak through books you may be reading and television shows you may be watching. Watch out for all of the synchronicities that you experience throughout your day. God is blessing you when you understand the messages from your angels. Letting them into your life will help you to know what messages they giving you. Watch out for feathers, no matter how big or small the feather may be. When you see one, the angels are letting you know they are around.

## Journal exercise:

Have you experienced getting an angel message through one of the ways mentioned above? Think about it and journal about it.

# April 18

Go deeply into your heart place where peace and love exist. Know that this is the place where your true spirit and essence live. We, your angels, ask you to spend time in this place, to be there during meditation for introspection and at other times when needed. Be sure to clear away the cobwebs and negative emotions that may be blocking you. This will help you to live easily in the heart place.

## Journal exercise:

What negative emotions do you need to clear from your heart place? Think about it and journal about it.

# April 19

Letting the past stay in the past and not thinking of the future until you get there makes it much easier to be in the present. Taking baby steps each moment you are awake to help form the future will help you not to dwell on the past…Living in the moment and enjoying each one helps to make life a pleasure. When you let go of negatives and live in the present instead, you can enjoy the journey of your life. Making each connection one of love and joy adds to your joy. Everybody's path is different, but we all have the same goals: love and happiness and success. Being open to everyone you meet and accepting who they are makes the path more enjoyable and exciting. Enjoy the journey, for you will certainly enjoy the goal when it's reached.

## Journal exercise:

Have you made any joyful connections recently? Think about it and journal about it.

# April 20

*Dear Angels,*

What message do you have for us today?

Healing and colors go together, no doubt about it. The colors each have different meanings and are paired with a chakra. The chakras are energy centers in your body; each chakra has a specific color associated with it. There are also different shades of each color, such as deeper or lighter shades of particular colors corresponding with each chakra. Sometimes there can be two or three shades of a color swirled together in a chakra. When healing yourself or giving healing to others, we, your angels, help you with the healing. Imagine there are long ribbons of color or maybe swirls of moving color. We can help you to know what colors are needed. They are used for calming and relaxing and also to guide you in going where healing is needed most. Don't be afraid to use color when doing a healing or when sending a healing.

There are so many different ways of healing that we know you are aware of. Another way is healing with stones or crystals. They come in different colors and can also be paired with a chakra. The crystals have different meanings and healing properties.

## Journal exercise:

What type of healing interests you? What types of healing have you experienced for yourself? What types of healing do you want to learn to use on others or to experience yourself? Think about it and journal about it.

# April 21

Living the life that you were meant to live is really in your own hands. Are you coming from a place of ego or the heart place? How you respond to what happens to you is your choice at any and all times. Response is an individual choice, for we all make different choices no matter what the day may bring. Living in your heart place helps you to steer straight and remain calm through whatever happens. Sometimes stepping back and taking quiet inventory of all aspects and sides of an issue helps you to respond in a healthy way. It is easy to fly off the handle, become hurt or angry or to ignore the events of the day. If you are in your heart place you will most likely ask your source or your angels, "How I can respond in a way that keeps me in the heart place?" We all know what it's like to react impulsively. Where does it take us? Yep, it's a release of emotion, but is it a healthy release? No one is perfect when reacting to charged issues in their daily life. We can make changes for the better when we respond from the heart place.

## Journal exercise:

What kinds of events provoke a negative response and how can you go from responding from the ego to responding from the heart place? Think about it and journal about it.

# April 22

Letting go of fears that don't serve you can be the most wonderful gift to yourself. It frees you from projecting what may not be true or may never happen. It helps you to focus on what is truly important. Sometimes our worst fears can take such a hold on us that we cannot focus on anything else. The angels say that when it comes to our worst fears, 99 percent of what we focus on is just not true in any way. They say that going to the heart place and meditating there is a good way to discern what is true and what isn't. Take some deep breaths and count to ten, and then write down what you are focusing on. Be still and ask for guidance in this matter. Listen to the answers and know that all is well.

## Journal exercise:

What fears are you focusing on today? How can the angels help you with them? Think about it and journal about it.

# April 23

Clinging to the past, for some, is like clinging to a black hole of memories that are no longer necessary to remember. For some of us, what we are clinging to in the past is what keeps us in our misery. Why not, right now, take steps to making our present days more pleasant and full of the things we want to see in our lives. Making the present as wonderful as possible will help the memories of the past start to become less important. This isn't an instant thing that can be done to make our past and present better right away. It's a start in doing this. Becoming grateful for all that you have helps in the process of making the past and present more pleasant.

As children, we didn't have any control of what our present and past was. We are adults now and we do have some control in thinking about how our past affected us and influences us in the present. It starts with how we decide to look at our past. It also depends on the attitude we take in the present. It seems to us, your angels, that when you have dealt with all in your past that your present can be more enjoyable and your future has a better chance of being just as wonderful as your present.

## Journal exercise:

What is one thing you can do today to focus on the present and let a bad memory start to fade? Think about it and journal about it.

# April 24

*Dear Children,*

What have done you done for yourself lately? What random act of kindness have you given to yourself? Have you treated yourself with something that will truly help you be in a place of complete bliss? We are aware that you have a hard time giving yourself a special treat. We want you to know you deserve to receive it. No matter how big or how small, it's the act of treating yourself well that is the main purpose of this special treat. We are mentioning this to give you some food for thought.

## *Journal exercise:*

What kind of special treat can you give yourself today or in the near future? Think about it and journal about it.

# April 25

Don't forget, my child, we are always here for you. Thank you for your patience in showing others how to come to us. We appreciate you sharing your knowledge of us with others. We want to help all who are interested in us. When you speak about us it helps others to know and understand us too.

## Journal exercise:

Have you talked about the angels? If so, what have you said about the angels to others? Think about it and journal about it.

# April 26

Be at peace, for clarity is coming soon. Let your concerns turn to knowing that all will be fine. Let the Universe take care of your worries and let it do what is needed for all to be right. Patience is needed, and trust is needed, so that you will understand why your vision is happening on the Universe's time table.

What vision do you have that is not manifesting on your time table? It is sometimes hard for those on the Earth plane to understand the Universe's reasons for manifesting their visions on its time table, which seems to be much slower than desired. The angels suggest taking note of all whom you meet on your path, and also what you hear on the television or the radio or in passing conversations. For these are all a part of the path you are traveling.

## Journal exercise:

What vision do you have that is not manifesting on your time table? Think about it and journal about it.

# April 27

"Child, do not panic at the confusion you may be feeling today. Let your worries be warnings that you may need to slow down and work at a slower pace. Let go of your worries for a time today and just be. Relax and tell us your concerns. We can only help if you ask for guidance. Take care of yourself and be at peace."

When you feel confusion, you feel as though as your life is falling apart and, when you feel panicked, it can be extremely overwhelming. Ask the angels for help and know that all is well.

## Journal exercise:

What is making you feel panicked at this time? What can you do to help yourself? Think about it and journal about it.

# April 28

Let your joy show today. Let the peace that is felt within your very core radiate out for all to see. Joy is a wonderful feeling and needs to be shown to all. Do not be afraid to do the dance of joy for all to see. Joy can be contagious. Just think, if we all showed our joy, how wonderful our world would be. Let your light shine. Today is a day of JOY. Celebrate!

## Journal exercise:

What makes you joyful? How can you share your joy today? Think about it and journal about it.

# April 29

Today open your hearts to all you meet and know. Hear the messages within your heart. Know that the clarity of these messages is what you need to hear today. Let the joy be felt wherever you go. Don't give up, no matter what, for we, your angels, are with you. Ask us for assistance and we will be with you.

## Journal exercise:

What can you ask the angels for help with today? Think about it and journal about it.

# April 30

Dear Child, to hear our words is to be open to possibilities. Know that the possibilities are endless. Know that we are here for you. Ask us to guide you during times of worry and times that are difficult. We will be here for you listening to all that concerns you.

## Journal exercise:

What would you like to speak to your angels about today? Think about it and journal about it.

# Living in the Heart Place
# with Your Angels

# May Messages

# May 1

Let the voices of spring touch your heart. Enjoy the beauty of the flowers blooming. Let the scenes of nature bring you peace. The newness of the season can give birth to new ideas. It's a perfect time to set some goals for this lovely season. Be happy and enjoy all that is happening now.

## Journal exercise:

What goals do you have for this month? What plans have you made? Think about it and journal about it.

# May 2

Choirs of Angels singing make this a day to be proud of and to celebrate the many gifts you have. Today don't hide all that you are; let your light shine to all whom you meet and may peace reign in your heart.

Be proud of who you are at all times. You are precious to the Universe. Don't be afraid of your truth for it is wonderful. The angels love you, always remember this.

## Journal exercise:

How can you let your light shine today? Think about it and journal about it.

# May 3

The essence of life is love. When we know this, we know that we have all that we need to survive in life. Love always makes our lives better and brighter. When you feel love, your light shines brightly to all who see you or are near you. Let your love shine to help those who need to feel the brightness of your soul. The light that is felt is like a warm sunny day. May all your days be sunny and bright.

Love and light are all that your heart truly needs in this life. The rest will take care of itself. When you feel love and shine your light to all whom you meet, your brightness is seen by all.

## Journal exercise:

How can you shine your light to all whom you meet today? Think about it and journal about it.

# May 4

Let your heart shout out for joy. Let your smile be of dreams come true. Know that the Universe is hearing you today. Let the joy and the dreams you have today become the realities of tomorrow. Let the clarity you feel in this endeavor help your wishes come true.

Look out for messages from your angels today. Know that they will provide clarity about something you need.

## Journal exercise:

What did your angels have to say to you today that helps your dreams come true? Think about it and journal about it.

# May 5

May your joy radiate to all whom you meet today. Let the sunshine in your heart shine on all whom you meet. Know that your pure intention is to live your truth and integrity. May those who need it hear your truth and feel its clarity. We, your angels, are here to help you shine light in all that you do. Let this light be the beacon that helps you to heal and to move through your day in a way that is pleasing to you. Love is the answer, this you know. When you choose love you know that the angels are near. Love is always present with your angels and your guardian angel, who is always close to you. Many Angel Blessings to you today.

Your guardian angel has been with you since birth and has watched over you all of this time. Do not be afraid to live your truth and let your light shine brightly so all can see the light that you are.

## Journal exercise:

How can you show to the world the love and bright light that you always are? Think about it and journal about it.

# May 6

When times are difficult and not going well, ask your angels for guidance. When you do this, you will know that you are not alone. Asking for our help will help you to focus on the issue. We, the angels, care and are listening to all of you. Sometimes when we wait, it means that at this point in the journey the Universe is helping in the background so that your vision and solution can come to fruition. We encourage you to enjoy the journey even if there are places that are difficult.

You have asked for help. Know that we are helping and working things out for you.

## Journal exercise:

Was there a time when you asked for help and the solution was slow in coming? Think about it and journal about it.

## May 7

Have you had a moment of inspiration when a wonderful idea has come into your mind? It could be an idea for a creative project or an idea of how to remodel a room in your home, or even an idea of how to bring more money into your life. The idea that came to you has not left your mind. As you think of the idea, it starts to grow and you think of all the possibilities for this new project. This is a perfect example of angel intuition and angelic guidance. When you start to become aware of this guidance from the angels, it will help you to see that the angels are truly working with you.

## Journal exercise:

What creative thoughts have you had recently? Is there one idea you would like to act on? Make a plan to carry this idea out. Think about it and journal about it.

# May 8

*Dear Children,*

Treasure the loved ones in your life. Let them know from time to time how important they are to you. Spend quality time with them and cherish this time. Let the joy of being with them show in the way you speak to them. Let them know how special they are. They may already know this but it's always nice to be told again. Remember, communication with those closest to you is important. Tact is important in this communication so that there will not be misunderstandings. Enjoy the time together and we, your angels, will rejoice in this too.

*Journal exercise:*

What is your favorite way to spend time with family and friends? Think about it and journal about it.

# May 9

Guardian Angels are angels who stay with you always. They watch out for you at all times. They are with you in times of joy, sadness, anger, laughter and peace. They help you to make your dreams come true. They warn you of danger or unsafe circumstances. Many times young children will speak to their Guardian Angels, calling them a friend, and then lose touch with them as they grow older. But guardian angels do not go away when you forget them or lose touch with them. They are always there for you, both in times of comfort and in times when hard lessons are being learned. Do not be afraid to call on your Guardian Angel. He or she is waiting for you to speak to him or her, right this minute!

## Journal exercise:

Try speaking to your Guardian Angel about what is on your mind tonight. What do you hear? What do you feel? What do you see? Journal about what transpired when you spoke with your Guardian Angel.

# May 10

Focus on all that is important to you at this time. Do not let negative energies sway you in a negative direction. When you ask us to help with this, we, your angels, will be glad to do so. Focus on the message of love and only love. We can show you the peace and clarity in all of this. Be grateful for all that you have and trust that the Universe is helping in every way.

When we know our truth and what is important to us, we know that where we are is where we need to be at this time. Don't be afraid to ask your angels for help. They will show you and guide you to make your truth and vision come to fruition.

## Journal exercise:

What project or truth needs help from your angels at this time? Think about it and journal about it.

# May 11

*Dear Children,*

Let your healing energy come through in a smile or a hug. Let the healing happen when you send healing thoughts to a friend who is in pain or sad. Healing is not something that is done by the "Healers". Everyone is a healer in his or her own right. A mom is a healer when she is being a mother. She may be giving advice or tending to an injury her child has. A teacher is a healer when she is helping her students to learn a new concept and helping them understand how to incorporate this into their life. There is care and passion in this instruction and it may help someone to feel empowered and grow in a positive way.

Healing is hands-on touch and pure intention to help this person by being a channel of God's love and energy. Healing can come from belief in a philosophy you choose to follow. Healing comes when you are listening to a friend who may be troubled and needs a listening ear. Healing can be engaging in art, such as painting. It can also be creating in other mediums, such as writing, journaling, composing poetry or writing a letter to someone you care for. There is also much healing in being out in nature and breathing fresh air and taking in beauty.

Healing is not a special power that a select few possess. Healing is contagious and it can be done by anyone. We are healing beings, it is at our core.

When healing is sent over a distance, with pure intention to the receiver, it's sent with love. If each of us sent our healing love to those in all parts of our world, think of what a bright beacon of light the world would be. We are all beacons of light and love, it's in our core and we can keep it bright by focusing on all that is good and positive. Let your light shine and be proud of who you are, for we are all healers each day in many different ways.

## Journal exercise:

Think about whom has been a healing presence in your life. Has it been a friend, a family member, a pet? Think about it and journal about it.

# May 12

Focus on a vision you have and let nothing get in the way. Dream your dreams and know they can be realities for you. Never give up, each person or place is part of the journey. We, your angels, ask you to enjoy the journey and to know that the dream is a work in progress. You can ask us for help and we will be there for you.

## Journal exercise:

Which dream are you hoping to realize at this time? The angels ask that you do not give up on hope, no matter how difficult this is. Think about it and journal about it.

# May 13

*Dear Children,*

We want you to know that we are here for you at all times. Tell us your issues so we can guide you to the right decisions. The decisions are ultimately yours. Your free will is always respected; we will not interfere in any way. Let your light shine both within and around you. Be at peace always.

Love,

Archangel Raphael and the Angels

## Journal exercise:

Is there something you would like to speak to Archangel Raphael about? Think about it and journal about it.

# May 14

Let today be the day you say, "I will do it." Let today be the day you say what you feel. Let today be the day you do what you intended to do. Let all your promises be truths and let the Universe help your dreams come true.

## Journal exercise:

To have a positive attitude toward all you want to do on a particular day is a great way to begin the day. What do you intend to do today to help your dreams come true? Think about it and journal about it.

# May 15

The sun is bright today, just as the light inside of you is shining brightly. Let the brightness guide you to all things that are good. Let the brightness of your light help guide your heart in making your dreams come true. We, your angels, can help with this. Remember this: the light in your heart shines always. Sometimes you smother your light with anger, resentment, sadness, egotism. Let your light shine no matter what. For when you shine your light in times of difficulty, it is what gets you through and your truth will prevail no matter what obstacles lie before you. Asking for a hand from the angels will make it less difficult.

## Journal exercise:

What do you need to let go of that is blocking your light? Writing about it helps to release it. Also ask Archangel Raphael for help in healing this negativity. Think about it and journal about it.

# May 16

Dealing with our deeper issues is like peeling an onion. The more we peel through the layers of the onion, the more tears come. Let the tears come and let them heal you down to the deepest layers. Do this until you feel the healing has reached deep within you. The more superficial layers will no longer be important. This is because healing has taken place and clarity and peace are deep within your core. Today the angels urge you to take care of yourself and know that they are by your side, helping you to feel the healing energy of their love.

## Journal exercise:

How have you felt the healing love of the angels and of God, today or in the past? Think about it and journal about it.

# May 17

Today, feel that there is a choir of angels around you and that they are sitting with you on the arm of your chair. Hear the sounds of nature as you walk outdoors. Listen to the songs of the birds, the buzzing of the bees and the chirping of the chipmunks. Watch the swaying of the trees and feel their cool breeze. When you walk by a babbling brook, listen to the sound as you follow it as far as you are able. When walking past beautiful flowers, breathe in deeply, noticing the different fragrances around you. Please enjoy all that is in Nature and be at peace with all that is. Nature is God's gift to all of us. Use it wisely.

## Journal exercise:

Where can you go today to enjoy nature? Think about it, go there if you can, and then journal about it.

# May 18

Be at peace today for all will be well. Feel the peace deep within you. As you hear the messages of the angels you will feel more clarity and understanding of what is happening. Know that they will always be with you. If doubt creeps into your mind, set it aside for it does not belong to you. Give it back to the Universe and know the angels will replace the doubt with trust.

## Journal exercise:

Have you had any angel messages recently that have given you clarity? Think about it and journal about it.

# May 19

Let the angel whispers you hear today be a comfort to you. Let the angels know you need to hear them. Do not be afraid to ask them questions, for they are waiting for you to speak with them at any time.

## Journal exercise:

The angels are with you; what questions do you have for them today? Think about it and journal about it.

## May 20

"Today we speak of being at peace and knowing that all is good. To have this clarity is to be free from what is not of the light. Being at peace means knowing that all is well. Thinking positively helps to more clearly plan your dreams and hopes for your lives and for those who are close to you."

Ask your angels for help with this. Read books that are uplifting and help you to understand what being in the light means. The more you surround yourself with positivity the more you will feel uplifted and happy. You will then feel peace.

## Journal exercise:

Think about ways you can be positive in your daily life. Think about it and journal about it.

# May 21

Be at peace for all will be well. Know that we, your angels, are close and that God too is close by your side. Let your fears fall away and let the worries you have today disappear from your thoughts.

Let the light in your heart shine for all to see. Ask that the light be for all and let love be there as well. When you think of it, light and love go together always. They are never separate. Know this to be true at all times.

## Journal exercise:

What fears do you have at this time that you would like to give to your angels? Think about it and journal about it.

# May 22

Children, know that we are with you today. Be at peace for now is the time to share your knowledge with all whom you know. You may be asking, "What am I to share?" We say to you, at this time share your light and share your love. Share the peace you feel today even if it is miniscule. Know that as you share, it will become larger. Keep your eye on your vision and your passion. Let your vision and your passion become large and become reality. Life is grand if you let it be that. We love you always.

## Journal exercise:

What do you know? What are you passionate about? Does it benefit others in some way? Think about it and journal about it.

# May 23

What does it take to find the peace you need to have for today? Just reach deep into your core and understand that it is already there for you. You have to peel away the stress, the strain, the negative thinking, and accept only positive thoughts along with clarity and serenity. Positive thoughts do bring happy thoughts and those happy thoughts bring you peace and calm. Let the happy thoughts spill over into pure happiness.

## Journal exercise:

Think of a place you would like to be, either that you know or that you have made up. Put yourself into this place, be happy, and see yourself at peace. Think about this place and then describe it in your journal.

# May 24

Today we are speaking of light and love. Light and love are the ingredients which make you into who you truly are. We all have light and we all have love that we show in varying degrees. Some of you may hide your light a bit when not feeling up to par, but it is there in full force waiting to be shown to the world. Love is at your very core, yet you may not feel it at different times. It is there and you will see it when you clear away layers of pain. Some of you have been hurt and broken, have even become numb. Know that the light within you and the love within you are still there for you to feel. You can ask us, your angels, especially Archangel Raphael, to help you to heal to your core. Positive affirmations help with this as well.

## Journal exercise:

Here is an affirmation to practice: "Today I am happy." Say it over and over, and see how it makes you feel, and if you can release your negative feelings more easily. Think about it and journal about it.

# May 25

Walking your path is not always easy. There may be many winding bends on the path. It can also be a little rocky. Please do not turn back on your path when this happens. Forge ahead and let the Universe take care of where it is all leading to. It all happens for a reason. Sometimes we do not see this and it is hard to get back on track. Ask the angels for help, for they really do want to help. Patience is key here. To stay patient and to keep your eye on your goal is paramount. Let the Universe worry about the problems you encounter.

You will always encounter mountains and valleys as you travel on your spiritual path. The key is to keep your eye on the vision you have for yourself.

## Journal exercise:

What valleys have you traveled into lately that have been difficult for you? Think about it and journal about it.

# May 26

Kayaking is a sport of balance. You cannot shift over too far on one side because you will tip over. It's all in the balance. Life needs to be balanced too. Too much work and no play is not a particularly healthy way to live. When this happens, we are off balance. Too much food and gaining weight keep us off balance as well. Too much alcoholic drink also keeps us off balance. Exercise and eating in moderation help us to stay in balance. A goods night's rest keeps us in balance. Being around people who are kind and pleasant keeps our lives and thoughts in balance. Meditation keeps us in balance. The angels want us to know it is all about the balance of life that keeps us steady and productive. The kayak is a perfect example of what balancing is and how we need balance to enjoy the ride that is our lives.

## Journal exercise:

Make a list of the practices you do that keep you in balance. Make a list of the activities that may be keeping you off balance. Prioritize the practices that keep you in balance. How can you use them to replace some of the ones that may be keeping you off balance? Think about it and journal about it.

# May 27

## Dear Angels,

What do you, the angels of the Universe, have to say to us today?

## Dear Children,

Let God and the angels help you with worries that take up a lot of time during the day. We ask you to please understand that we take each concern seriously. We will help you in any way that is possible. We celebrate your joys too and rejoice with you. Ask for guidance when you have questions and we will help you in the best way we can.

## Journal exercise:

What do you want the angels to help you with today? Think about it and journal about it.

# May 28

Focus on a dream you want to realize in your life. Let the dream be a reality for you. Know that we, your angels, are helping it to come to fruition. We say this often, but please enjoy the journey that you are traveling. The path will not be boring, we promise you this. Each step of the path will bring something new, something special and very memorable. You are all on different paths with different visions, yet your goals are the same—peace, love, happiness, to have a good job, and so on. Accept and share with each other the differences of your visions. It would be very boring if all of you had the same experiences on your paths. Celebrate your uniqueness. Celebrate your lives.

## Journal exercise:

This is so true: we are all on the same path and yet each path is different. When we look at our own path and the path a close relative or friend is on, they truly are different. How do you see this in your own life? Think about it and journal about it.

# May 29

Create a place in your home where you can sit and be still. A place that is full of peace, and where you can meditate. Listen to the whispers that you hear. What are they saying and what are you feeling? We, your angels, are here for you and we will guide you when you ask us to. The ball is in your court.

## Journal exercise:

Today sit in your quiet place and try to hear the subtle voices. Speak to the angels, for they will speak to you. What will you ask the angels? What do they say to you? Think about it and journal about it.

# May 30

Hearing the songs of the birds and smelling the scents of the flowers when we walk outdoors, and feeling the cool breeze, help us to see the beauty of nature and our natural surroundings. We are all so blessed with whatever parts of nature surround us. Find a place of beauty to be around. Take in the beauty and be at peace.

## Journal exercise:

What things in nature interest you? Think about it and journal about it.

# May 31

Pay attention to the lessons you receive each day for they are for learning and understanding your life's path. Taking baby steps is okay. It helps you to see your progress. Be sure to know and understand that there are bends in the trail and sometimes the trail can be tricky. Each step you make, though small, is a major step towards the vision you and your angels have for you.

## Journal exercise:

Think about and write about the progress you have made in the past month. Put an accent on the positive and then give the negative to the Universe.

# Living in the Heart Place
## with Your Angels

## June Messages

# June 1

Today the angels say that blessings are abundant for all. We all have a wealth of things to be thankful for. Try making a list each day of all that you are grateful for. Thanking the angels and God for the abundance in your life at this time is a wonderful way to acknowledge their help in all that is happening in your life.

## Journal exercise:

What do you have to be grateful for today? Think about it and journal about it.

# June 2

Summertime is soon upon us. The butterflies are dancing their dance from flower to flower. As springtime leads into summer, the flowers continue to bloom and the gardens start to produce healthy food for all. How lucky are we to experience this lush bounty! It is a time of planning summer activities in the water and in the mountains, planning family travel and time to be together. We, your angels, ask you to plan wisely and to make this time safe for all.

## Journal exercise:

What do you like best about spring and summer? Think about it and journal about it.

# June 3

## Dear Children,

Please know that we, your angels, are here for you when times get tough. Know that we see all that is happening in your world. We are here to help in difficult times and will comfort and guide all who seek our help. We will not leave you in times of hardship. We are by your side. Today let your light shine and share it with others. The world needs your light to survive. Think of what could happen if everyone let their lights shine to the brightest extent always. The bright lights of all would keep your planet in the higher vibration of spiritual light always.

## Journal exercise:

How can you let your light shine today to all whom you meet? Think about it and journal about it.

# June 4

When you hear our whispers, you will know it is us, your angels, because we speak softly and in very subtle tones. If you have a thought that is not usually yours, yet it is a positive thought, take note of it. Let your fears dissipate for we are close by your side. Today we ask you to try this when you meditate. We are waiting for you.

## Journal exercise:

What thoughts lately have you had that were subtle yet positive? Think about it and journal about it.

# June 5

We, the angels, would like you to know that you are loved. We ask that you believe this and share this knowledge with others. We, the angels and God, are on your side and will guide you to your vision. We say this so many times, yet we wonder if you truly hear us. Do you know that when you walk around in a special place such as a beach, a mountain top, or even a beautiful park, the Universe is whispering to you? Listen, for it whispers to you in your heart. Listen to what you have not heard before that makes sense. Listen to what may be a validating thought, to assure you to go ahead with your plan. Everyone likes validation. Everyone also likes collaboration. We are your collaborators and we will listen to all you have to say or ask. Do not forget God is our maker and loves each one of us and we, your angels, are your guidance along with all that is in the Universe. Do not waste time with thoughts that are negative, when thoughts that are positive are so much more enlightening. Be at peace and know you are loved.

## Journal exercise:

Look at all of the beauty around you. What whispers have you heard lately deep within? Think about it and journal about it.

# June 6

The angels are letting you know they are with you and they feel your happiness as well as your sadness. They remind you to let your light shine brightly to all.

## Journal exercise:

How can you know your angels are with you always? Think about it and journal about it.

# June 7

The Angels have this to say today:

## Dear Children,

We are pleased that you are reaching out to us and asking for our guidance. We are pleased that your light is shining brightly to all whom you meet. Please continue to shine your light all around. Please continue to spread the word about the choirs of angels who are around at all times. So many people don't understand about their angels and how the angels want to help them. By your actions and examples, others will see the truth of what you have been saying. Let your light shine brightly; let your heart, not your ego, be who you show to the world. We know you can do this and we know that you will come to us for help with this.

## Journal exercise:

How can you help others get to know the angels when they ask you about them? Think about it and journal about it.

# June 8

Go forth and help to heal all who are suffering today. Bring them food, and bring them water. Light workers help to heal all who suffer. Let your voices assure them that all is fine and that they are alright. Let your light shine for all who are in need of pure intent and clarity. Be at peace for you now have clarity in all that is felt today. When you focus on the positive, you are letting your light shine for those to see. Be free, be happy, and be of the light. We love you and we will help you always.

## Journal exercise

What are some of the ways we can help others who are suffering? How can we make them comfortable and help them to feel some hope? Think about it and journal about it.

# June 9

*Dear Children,*

Peace is a feeling in your hearts, down to the very core, where you feel clarity about all you are experiencing now. Sometimes this is easy for you to see and sometimes it is hard. Know that when you look deep within your core, that is where love is and that love is where the light you are is. Realize that the light you shine is indeed the light of God. God is within all of us and God's light will bring true happiness and peace to you. We ask you to be patient with understanding this feeling of God's light, because it is something you all possess. Positive affirmations can help with this and bolster your heart in feeling this way.

## *Journal exercise:*

What kind of affirmations will help you to feel at peace and happy to the core of your being? Can you write down one to three? How else can you let the light in and be at peace? Think about it and journal about it.

# June 10

Abundance comes in so many ways. It can be an abundance of friends, or an abundance of material things or spiritual abundance. We suggest that you take stock of the types of abundance that are in your life. The Law of Attraction speaks of abundance as energy when referring to money. When you wish to acquire abundance monetarily, you must think and speak of this in a positive way and then let the Universe bring it to you. Letting go of trying to control this outcome is so difficult, but keep your eye on your vision. Do the footwork and remain positive in all ways, knowing that your vision will happen. Remain grateful despite the appearance of lack and bring positive energy to your vision. Something to remember is that the timing of this manifestation happens on the Universe's own timetable. We encourage you to put your request out to the Universe and to enjoy the journey of how this all comes to fruition. Take note of whom you meet and the opportunities that come to you during your journey, for the angels are helping your dream come true.

## Journal exercise:

What types of abundance are you blessed with? Think about it and journal about it.

# June 11

The best is yet to come. We say this because you are waiting patiently for something and know that it all happens in its own good time, and not always when you planned for it to happen. We are helping to manifest this vision and we are with you.

## Journal exercise:

What vision do you have at this time that you are patiently waiting to manifest? Is there something else that you have asked for that you are waiting for? Think about it and journal about it.

# June 12

Come into your heart place. Feel the peace and clarity that are there. Let the clarity help you discern the right path for you. Ask your angels to help you and they will. Let the truth you live be the truth of who you truly are.

## Journal exercise:

Finding your heart place is an interesting way to find your peace. How do you do this? Think about it and journal about it.

# June 13

The Angels ask you today to be at peace when it seems hardest to do so. They ask you to know that this too will pass and you can continue your journey. Feel the negative feelings, then give them to the Universe, for you have no use for them. You can find a better route to a positive way of being. As you walk on your path in the days to come you will understand the reason for all of these events. We urge you to look beyond this hard time and we ask you to continue the journey as you have always done.

## Journal exercise:

Sometimes waiting is hard after asking the Universe for help. Enjoy each step of your journey and see how the progression of your vision starts to fall into place. Think about it and journal about it.

## June 14

Let your fears be given to us, your angels. Do not let the fears paralyze you and prevent you from taking the next step. Know we are carrying you to safety and will let no harm come to you. Let peace and clarity prevail for we will not leave you. We love you dearly, child, never forget this. Give us your burden for it is not in your hands. Look to the light and know that all is fine with you.

### Journal exercise:

The angels are asking you to feel safe for they are here with you at this time. How does it feel to trust them and feel safe? Think about it and journal about it.

# June 15

Children, never doubt our love for you. Listen to your hearts and be at peace, for we are here with you, ready to listen whenever you want to speak to us. Be clear about what help you would like with your goals.

## Journal exercise:

What goal would you like to ask the angels for help with today? Think about it and journal about it.

# June 16

## Dear Angels,

What would you like us to know today?

There will be times that will be difficult, but know that we are here for you to show you how to continue on your path. We will be with you as you learn the ins and outs of all that is occurring. We will carry you over the times that are scary and share your glory in times of happiness. We ask you to be patient and to know we are here. Today we ask that you take notice of who is on your path with you and know that we are guiding you to meet who you need to have in your life.

## Journal exercise:

Who have you met on your path lately who will help your progress on your spiritual journey? Think about it and journal about it.

# June 17

*Hello Dear Children,*

We want to speak about the light that you shine when you are in your truth. Your truth tells the world, "I am me and I will not be swayed by you unless your truth is close to my truth. I respect your truth and understand your truth, but it is not my truth. So please respect me as I respect you in all that you do." Letting your light shine as you let others shine their light is a form of peaceful respect for all. We ask this of all of you, because respect of one another's truth is the way to peace. In this way we say we are all of one mind, yet we have different ways of expressing it.

*Journal exercise:*

What was an experience you had when your truth was not accepted by another? How did you feel about this and were you able to let the differences be accepted and respected? Think about it and journal about it.

# June 18

Today slow down and go at a slower pace in all you are doing. Try meditating or taking a walk. Try cleaning your home or office, one room at a time. Let your light shine brightly in all that you do today. Be at peace.

The angels ask you to be slow today and to take time for you.

## Journal exercise:

What would you like to do at a slower pace today? Think about it and journal about it.

# June 19

*Dear Children,*

Let your hearts shout with love and with light. Let the light shine within and all around you. Do not fear the future, look to the moment. When you live in the moment you are not living in the past, nor are you looking to the future. This way, living in the now is what your attention is focused on. Do not fear nor doubt what the future is to be, nor think of the past. Let events come together and know that all will make sense to you in time. Enjoy the journey.

## *Journal exercise:*

Living in the now can be very scary. We are so busy thinking of the past or the future. Try sitting and thinking about what is happening now. Just be in the moment. How does that feel? Think about it and journal about it.

# June 20

Let the peace in your heart be there at all times for you. Let this peace help you to live each day in a place that is positive and full of clarity. Focus on all that will allow your light to shine. Your angels are with you always. Know that they will help you when you ask.

## Journal exercise:

How can you let your light shine at all times? Think about it and journal about it.

# June 21

What would you like to hear from us, your angels, today? We want to let you know that you are loved by us. We will not abandon you in any way. Ask us for help and we will be there for you. Try to live in the moment and not look to the future nor back to the past. We will help you to make miracles happen. You can help these miracles to occur through positive thinking. Do not be afraid.

Asking us for help is a good way for your hopes and dreams to be realized.

## Journal exercise:

What would you like to ask the angels for help with today? Think about it and journal about it.

# June 22

*Dear Children,*

Do not be afraid of what you are capable of. Know that your gifts will carry you through at all times. Your gifts are from God and He will help you to develop them. Being at peace with this knowledge will help you to grow and flourish. We, your angels, say you can shoot for the moon. Go forward and be happy with all that you are doing.

## Journal exercise:

You have been given so many gifts by God. Today concentrate on one gift. How can you manifest it? Think about it and journal about it.

# June 23

Let peace reign in your heart. May you always be at peace even when it is hard to feel peaceful. This is your greatest test. When you can let feelings that are negative just pass by, then you know you have grown on your path. It is important to look at the feelings objectively and then to let them pass by. As the feelings pass by, you will begin to feel deep peace within your heart and you will feel joy after they are gone. Dear children, we, your angels, can help with this. We can show you the way to a joyful existence, for we are here for you always. "If God has brought you to it, he can bring you through it."

## Journal exercise:

Think of a time in your life when you have felt that you could not find peace. How were you eventually able to let the negative feelings pass and to let joy and peace back into your heart? Think about it and journal about it.

# June 24

## Dear Children,

When things are not clear, trust that the cloudiness will clear very soon. Patience is the main theme here and as you see divine timing occur, you will see your life play out as it is meant to. Know that the clouds do dissipate in time. We ask you to keep your eye on the vision that you have for your goal and don't give up. We ask that you show up for life and that you plan daily activities accordingly. This also helps to bring more clarity.

## Journal exercise:

What are some ways you can keep your focus on your vision right now? Think about it and journal about it.

# June 25

*Dear Children,*

We come to you today to say we love what you doing on the Earth plane. We feel that you are banding together with good intentions all around. Know that we are here to help you and that our messages help you to find your way. Let go of the belief "I am not worthy." Everyone is worthy and everyone has a different voice in all that they are doing. Don't be afraid if your message is a bit different from others, we will help you to present it in a positive way.

## Journal exercise:

Do not be afraid to speak the truth of what your beliefs are. Do you know what your truth and beliefs are today? Think about it and journal about it.

# June 26

*Dear Children,*

Let the celebration of the day be a high point for you. May all your days be full of high points. Concentrate on the positive and let positive feelings be a part of you. For you are full of brightness, light and love. All three can bring you the same things. Let no one tell you otherwise for we are all children of God.

## *Journal exercise:*

How can you concentrate on the positive things that your life is full of? How can you celebrate today? Think about it and journal about it.

# June 27

Focus on your path and think of all whom you have met on your trail of making your vision a reality. Continue to take note of your experiences to help you see how your dream is manifesting. Think of the experiences as stepping stones on the path. The trail will be rocky and it will be uphill and downhill, winding and bending. Yet you know that the trail is solid, and it will bring you to where you need to be. So be at peace with the result. Your angels are with you always and they will guide you through the difficult places. Embrace all parts of the journey. Your angels know you can do this.

## Journal exercise:

You know that there are many difficulties in your life. How can the angels help you on your path to make the journey smoother for you? Think about it and journal about it.

# June 28

When you have forgiveness in your heart, you are allowing each party to move on and to feel at peace. It allows you to travel different paths than you would otherwise and to have new opportunities come to you. Forgiveness will always clear the way forward. It will help to bring peace to your heart and let the light shine more brightly once again.

## Journal exercise:

Forgiveness is so important to help us to move on. What one thing today would you like to move on to? Think about it and journal about it.

# June 29

Let your light shine brightly and let the love of your angels always be there for you. They will help you have the clarity that you need in your life. Bring happiness to all whom you meet and let the love in your heart always be there for others.

## Journal exercise:

How can you let your light shine today? Think about it and journal about it.

# June 30

Feel the summer wind on your head. Feel the warmth of the summer sun upon your shoulders and your face. Feeling nature close to you brings you to a feeling of oneness with the natural world. Know that you are a child of God, loved unconditionally. Remember this, for you are precious.

## Journal exercise:

How does it feel to know you are a child of God and that He loves you unconditionally? Who have you loved unconditionally in your life? Think about it and journal about it.

# Living in the Heart Place with Your Angels

# July Messages

# July 1

Create a time and a place for you to meditate. This is a place where you can be at one with your Higher Power. If you like, you can put on soft music and light a candle. As you sit in a comfortable chair, know that your angels are with you. You can hear their words of wisdom and feel their love for you. Listen for the validating messages that you have needed to hear. They are helping you to see the validity of your vision. Be at peace, all is well.

## Journal exercise:

Quiet time is important to schedule into your day, even if it's only five minutes. What can you do to schedule this time for you? Think about it and journal about it.

# July 2

Ask in your heart, what is the most important thing to do for yourself? We, your angels, ask you this question because we feel that when you know the answer you will know the next step on your journey. When you know the answer you will not need to be concerned about other peoples' opinions and views of the angels. We ask you to stay in your truth and to do for yourself what you do for others. Let your vision be the goal point of your journey and know that all is well.

## Journal exercise:

Ask yourself, "What is the most important thing to do for myself?" Take some time to answer this. Think about it and journal about it.

# July 3

What message do you have for us?

Today, dear children, we would like to speak of truth and integrity. Integrity is when we live our truth. Do you live your truth? When you live your truth you have a sense of pride in who you are and have a feeling of peace and clarity of who you truly are, too.

## Journal exercise:

What is your truth today? Think about it and journal about it.

# July 4

Reach deep into your heart and see how you are doing at this time. Are you in a good place? Are you in a place of clarity? Have you found that you are feeling happy at this time? Let these feelings come to the forefront and let them guide you to who you need to be at this time. Let your light shine no matter what, even if you are in a place of difficulty. Let the light be your beacon for all to see you at your best. Your angels are with you at all times, as is God. Know this always.

## Journal exercise:

How are you feeling today? Can you feel the light that is deep within? Think about it and journal about it.

# July 5

Angels are all around us. They are helping us to grow into who we are truly meant to be. We can hear Angel Whispers throughout the day, helping us on our path. Angel Whispers are something we will always remember. The angels never let us go astray. Angels are leading us to pray. Thank you, angels, for your love, all throughout our day.

## Journal exercise:

What whispers did you hear from your angels today? Think about it and journal about what you heard today.

# July 6

*Dear Children,*

Let the peace you feel deep within your heart speak to the people you come into contact with each day. When you do not feel the peace, know that the angels can help you with this. We, your angels, want you to know that we never tire of helping you. So do not be afraid to ask.

## *Journal exercise:*

Have you thought about what type of assistance you would like to receive from your angels today? Think about it and journal about it.

# July 7

Letting in love from all around you is a gift you give to yourself. There is so much love surrounding you today. Let today's sunshine warm your heart as you let it in. The angels are with you today and always. Ask them to show you how they are with you at all times.

## Journal exercise:

Have you felt love from your angels yet today? Try meditating about the love around you and truly feel the love from your angels. Think about it and journal about it.

# July 8

Today we, your angels, want to speak to you about priorities. Sometimes you have so much to do that you are overwhelmed. You do not know where to turn or how to start with all that piles up on you. We suggest making a list and going through it each day, crossing off the finished tasks and going on to the next. The list helps you to have a positive attitude and to be organized. When you are organized, then you can see the end to the pile of things that need to be done. In addition, when you see the list getting shorter then you feel so much better. You know that all is going to be accomplished in the time needed for it to be finished. Ask Archangel Jophiel for help, as he loves to help with organization.

## Journal exercise:

What can you ask Archangel Jophiel to help you with today? He is waiting for you to ask for assistance. Think about it and journal about it.

# July 9

*Dear Angels,*

What do you have to say to us today?

Children, let your hearts rejoice in who you are and what your message is for others. Know that we are here to help you with your messages. When your love shines through in all you do, know that it has a positive effect on all around you. Be at peace with who you are and know that we are behind you in this. Forget about your fears and know that life is grand!

*Journal exercise:*

Our angels want to help us at all times. They also want to help us get our message out to others. They encourage us to let our light shine no matter how hard it may be at this time. How can you let your light shine to all whom you meet? How can you get your message out to all? Think about it and journal about it.

# July 10

*The angels say:*

Come to us, children, oh come to sing, sing out your joy. Come and be at peace, the peace you so deserve and will always get from us. We are in your corner and care for you, so you never need be upset. We hear your pleas and we are here for you.

*Journal exercise:*

How does it feel to know that the angels are in your corner helping you every step of the way? Think about it and journal about it.

# July 11

Don't be afraid to show your light everywhere you go. The light that you possess is powerful beyond your understanding of who you are. The light of the Universe is huge and we, your angels, want you to know of its power and of its goodness. Our light is the same and our gifts show us this. Don't be afraid of your power and use it well for all with whom you come into contact. Listen to the whispers within and know that your Angels, Guides and God are with you always. Rejoice in who you are.

## Journal exercise:

How can you show your light in your work and your play? Think about it and journal about it.

# July 12

We, your angels, greet you with much love. We will never leave you to suffer. We want to help. Don't be afraid to ask for help. How can we help you today? Do not be afraid to speak of your truth. For when you do this we will help you to speak your truth with much love and guidance.

## Journal exercise:

When the angels say they want to help us speak our truth, they are speaking of a positive message with pure intentions. Think of a positive message that you may have for all you know and want to help. Think about it and journal about it.

# July 13

The feathers that you find as you walk along are signs that your angels are ever so close. Know that feathers, whether big or small, are signs that we, your angels, are listening very closely and that we are near. Let this be a reminder of our love for you. You are always on our minds, feather or no feather. Keep the feathers and remember each time that you found one and what the circumstances were. They will make sense to you as time travels by. Know that we care for you and that your happiness is most important to us. We send you much love.

Have you ever found a feather that came to you at the exact time you needed to know your angels were near you? Take it as a sign from your angels.

## Journal exercise:

Write about the feathers that have found their way to be near you. Think about it and journal about it.

# July 14

*Dear Children,*

Enjoy the days that are seasonably comfortable and try to be out in nature to enjoy it. Go for walks along a path, on the beach or walk through the woods. Ride a bike, row a boat, go for a sail or walk to the top of a mountain.

## Journal exercise:

There are so many ways to enjoy nature. What is your favorite way? Think about it and journal about it.

# July 15

Look to us, your angels, for help on the Earth plane. We will be glad to help you. Prioritize what is important for you while you are in this life. Know that God is with you and we are there for you as well. Let the love in your heart direct you to wonderful people, places and things. Know that we are here for you at all times.

## Journal exercise:

Your angels are letting you know that you are not alone even when you feel that way. They encourage you to find the love in your heart, for that will always direct you to wonderful happenings in your life. How has this manifested in your life? Think about it and journal about it.

# July 16

Did you know that Archangel Raphael is the angel to help you with all healing work? He will also help you with the personal healing you are going through at this time. He will guide you gently to the core of the issue and help the healing to happen. He will help you find clarity in your healing and your healing work. There is one thing that you need to know. You have to *ask* for help when you would like assistance from him. He is waiting for you to speak to him but he respects your free will as all angels do. AA (Archangel) Raphael works a lot with AA Michael and together they help with healing and keeping you safe at all times.

## Journal exercise:

How can Archangel Raphael help you at this time with a concern that needs some healing? Think about it and journal about it.

# July 17

*Dear Children,*

Don't lose hope when life seems to be on a downward turn. We are with you and we will guide you to peace and clarity about what is happening at this time. Things are taken away so that the new can be given. We ask you to keep the faith. Know your truth and integrity in all of this. We will not abandon you in any way. We feel your pain and we feel your happiness. We want you to know that we are here for you always. There are different ways that you can stop your worrying. One is to write positive affirmations and put them on the mirrors of your home. Another is to write a letter to your favorite angel or even a letter to God. After you have written the letter, you can write a letter that is an answer from your favorite angel or God. Going out into nature also helps. Sitting in a garden or sitting by water can help lift your mood as well.

*Journal exercise:*

Write a letter to your favorite angel or God and then have them write a letter back. Put this in your journal.

# July 18

When you have peace and love in your heart, you will also feel clarity. By this we, your angels, mean that you will not have any negative thoughts and you will have peace of mind. We ask you to consider this. There are so many ways to feel peace and love in your heart. You can say positive affirmations aloud. Singing is a great way to feel happy and peaceful as well as being around people who are positive. When you are feeling sad, angry or depressed at any time, think of the feelings as a fog that has not lifted yet. You will know that when the fog has lifted or gone away, then the peaceful and calm feelings return. Know that it is a process and the outcome will be good. By just letting feelings pass by like fog does, you will still feel peace deep within you, because you know that the feelings have to be felt somewhat as they pass by.

## Journal exercise:

When you are feeling angry or depressed or another negative feeling, can you let the feeling pass by? Think about it and journal about it.

# July 19

When you worry too much about a request you have made, you are not letting the Universe do the work it needs to do. Let the Universe decide the timing and the order in which your request will be fulfilled. The timetable of the Universe is not the same as your timetable. Doing the footwork and making an effort in seeing your vision come to fruition will help the request be fulfilled. It may not be exactly what you have envisioned, but it is what the Universe knows is your best option. Keep track of whom you meet and who has helped you. They often have a piece of what you need to help your vision come true.

## Journal exercise:

What concern have you given to the Universe that you would like to have manifested a bit faster? Think about it and journal about it.

# July 20

Your free will is always honored when working with us, your angels. We will not contact you at any time unless you ask us for guidance or in a dire emergency. You will know we are around when you see different synchronicities happening in your life. You may see a feather or you may hear something on the phone, on the radio, on the television or in a conversation that are signs the angels are close to you. Synchronicities are such things as someone saying the same thing you were thinking at the same time or someone calling on the phone and you know who it is before answering. Other examples of synchronicities are being saved from a passing car swerving on the road or falling down and feeling like you are being held and falling ever so gently. Or you hear or feel within yourself a message like "pay a certain bill" or "don't go down this road". These are signs that your angels are helping you.

## Journal exercise:

What types of synchronicities have occurred for you lately? Think about it and journal about it.

# July 21

Angels are around you and keeping you calm. Angels are helping you to feel the peace within your heart. Let the angels take care of your worries and let them help to show you the way to positive outcomes. When the angels guide you to safety and peace know that Archangel Michael is there for you, along with your guardian angel. Archangel Raphael is with you also. He is helping you to heal the pain that is in your heart and he will replace the pain with unconditional love and healing.

## Journal exercise:

Isn't it nice to know that your angels are with you at all times? Is there something you want to ask your angels today? Think about it and journal about it.

# July 22

Let peace be within your being and within your heart. Let this be the thing that softens the pain and helps you to live life a little bit more joyously. Let the sorrow that you feel melt into love and let it go, for love is there beneath the sorrow. Love helps to melt all that is sad and all that is difficult. We, your angels, are here to help the love melt negative thoughts and emotions. We will guide you slowly to let your love melt in love, peace and clarity.

Let your love direct you to the highest place for love is grand. Our love will help you with this. Love makes you smile. Smiles are contagious. May today and its entire events make you smile, so that you feel the love, too.

## Journal exercise:

What makes you smile today? Think about it and journal about it.

# July 23

## Dear Children,

Today we are praising you for all you have done on the Earth plane. Each one of you, in your own way, has shown love toward someone on the Earth plane. Someone is an understatement, and we all know this. We know that you have shown your love to many on the Earth plane as you have been helping others to understand the events that have been and are taking place at this time. Try not to look back on the past and not to look too far into the future. Try to concentrate on what you can do now to help others. So many of your messages are so beautiful and so many of you have helped others to see what is happening now. You are light workers and you are helping us to help all on the Earth plane. Changes are coming in ways that are positive for everyone. Keep in tune with us and listen to your heart, because that is where your love is for others and for yourself. Celebrate all that is positive and all that is helping others to understand what is happening. We love you dearly and we thank you for your help. Namaste and angel blessings to all.

## Journal exercise:

How do you help out in the world as a light worker? Think about it and journal about it.

# July 24

Bless all of you who are with us on our journey. We thank you for your support each day. The word is getting out that we, the angels, exist and are here to help humankind to make the changes necessary for growth and rejuvenation. Don't be afraid to ask for help. Let the joy in your heart help you to grow. For this joy will spill into love for all to see. Do not be afraid to show your light to those whom you meet. Love comes in all different colors like the chakras:

Love comes in red, which can be a bit boisterous

Love comes in orange, which is deep and bright

Love comes in yellow, which is sunny and bright like a sunny day

Love comes in green, which can be a healing love from within

Love comes in blue, telling others about your love for them

Love comes in indigo, seeing the big picture of your love for all people

Love comes in purple, loving all things spiritual and understanding the messages of the Universe

## Journal exercise:

What color is your love today? Think about it and journal about it.

# July 25

If you could go anywhere in the world, where would it be? Whom would you see? What would you do? We ask you these questions for a reason. It has to do with how you can make your dreams come to fruition. Dreams are powerful, and they can come true. Write them down and prioritize them and keep your vision on them. Then it's a matter of letting the Universe manifest these dreams. Keep your thoughts positive and watch the miracles our Universe can make happen.

## Journal exercise:

What dreams do you have for yourself today that you would like to see manifested with help from the Universe? Think about it and journal about it.

# July 26

When we speak our truth, we speak from our heart. We speak our peace to those who question us. When we are questioned, at times our doubts about our truths sneak in. Let these doubts pass by like the fog of sadness or unhappiness. As they pass by, ask your true self, "Are these doubts the truth or are they just the ego blocking the truth? Do they serve me at this time?" Then ask yourself: "How can I put the truth in a positive light without any doubts?" We, your angels, ask you to try this each time doubt and ego come up for you when you are not being seen for who you are.

## Journal exercise:

Ask your angels and your guides for help if you have a hard time understanding this concept. Think about it and journal about it.

# July 27

## Dear Children,

Our wish for you today is to let you know that you are very much loved by us, your angels. We will be close by you if you need us for any reason. Enjoy your day, and the people that you will meet. Keep smiling on the inside and on the outside. We wish you many Angel Blessings throughout your day.

## Journal exercise:

Did you find time to speak with your angels today? Think about it and journal about your day.

# July 28

When you feel the light of God in your heart, know that all is well. When you feel the light of God, you will feel the clarity of God's plan for you. Through prayer and meditation, this will come to you clearly. God is with us all and He will help us and guide us in our divine plan. Never doubt this, for it is true He is with us and keeping us safe, with the help of our angels who are God's messengers. God's love is unconditional and He loves us all no matter what. The angels love us unconditionally too. How great is it that we are so loved? We do not always see it that way, especially when we think something negative has happened to us. This is the true test for some....When we think of it sometimes we feel that God has done us wrong, yet this is not true because everything happens with divine timing. This is hard for us to understand. God is the timekeeper, not us...Someday we will understand this too.

## Journal exercise:

What can you do to keep your dream alive and enjoy the journey while waiting on God's divine timing? Think about it and journal about it.

# July 29

Let the thorn in your heart dissolve to nothing. Fill the nothing space with something positive. For example, fill it with love, happiness or gratitude. Let this space be full of pinks and greens, which are colors of love and healing. Let it be filled with peace at all times. The angels tell us continually of their love for us and that they are with us, no matter what.

## Journal exercise:

Look daily for signs of love from the angels. They are there for you no matter how big or how small your problems may be. Think about it and journal about it.

# July 30

Tell us what is on your mind. Do not be afraid for we, your angels, will help when asked. We will not predict the future, or tell you what to do, for you have free will. We guide you on your path, but never forcefully. We respect you and treat you accordingly. We ask you to be at peace with this and know that we are never far away.

## Journal exercise:

What is on your mind today for which you want some guidance from your angels? Think about it and journal about it.

# July 31

Children, we are here to help you to understand the activities and events that are happening on the Earth plane at this time. There is much activity and it can be hard to watch, as there are many suffering in one way or another. We ask you to be patient and to help when given the opportunity to do so. The easiest thing you can do is to be helpful and loving towards people around you.

## Journal exercise:

What can you do today to help those suffering in some way? Think about it and journal about it.

# Living in the Heart Place with your Angels

# August Messages

# August 1

You have the ability, with the help of God, to be the co-creator of your life. You may be a bit curious about how you can become aware of this. A good start is to write down exactly how you want a certain vision to turn out and then ask God and the Universe to help you. See what happens, notice the people you are talking with, notice the books that are being spoken about. Be at peace; know that God, the Universe and the angels are helping you.

## Journal exercise:

How are you co-creating your dream today? Think about it and journal about it.

# August 2

*Dear Children,*

We are here to talk to you about belief. By belief, we mean the full acceptance of a concept that you agree with. We ask you to consider the concept of believing in yourself. So many times, we think that everyone has to believe what we believe or our truth is not worth stating. We want you to know that what you believe or the truth that you are is worth believing. We feel that living this way takes a lot of inner strength. We would like to see all people living in peace with each other no matter what anyone's beliefs are. To appreciate other people's beliefs and to not make judgments about their beliefs is very important for peace of mind and world peace. Each belief has its own merits and all beliefs need to be tolerated.

## Journal exercise:

What is a belief you have that someone else might not agree with? Why or why not? Think about it and journal about it.

# August 3

## Dear Children,

Imagine being in the middle of a large room filled with people talking to each other and realizing you are all alone and that no one is speaking to you. You realize this and feel very embarrassed. You hear a loud, critical voice saying, "How can you not be speaking to anyone?" You look around the room and think, "I am so embarrassed." Yet deep within your heart-core you hear a soft, comforting voice. You hear, "Be at peace for you are loved." You think, 'What have I just heard?" Then you hear music, soft and clear, and the song is "Let It Be", by the Beatles. You go to the restroom and when you come back an old friend you haven't seen in many years comes over to you and says hello. Your face lights up and you do not feel so alone anymore. You realize this has been the best party in a long time and your friend has a connection for a job that might be worth looking into.

We share this little story because we are showing you how the ego can wreak havoc with you when the critical and negative self-talk starts. Yet when you go deep within your inner core you can muffle the negative talk and hear the voices of your angels and watch the synchronicity take place. Your negative self-talk can lessen your self-confidence, especially when you just accept it as the truth about yourself. Ask us for guidance to help you through this. We want to help. We love you always.

## Journal exercise:

Have you ever had the experience of being alone in a room full of people? What happened? Think about it and journal about it.

# August 4

*Dear angels,*

What message do you have for us today? Let your light shine and let your voice be free, for we will give you the words that you need to express. Don't ever doubt our presence and guidance. We come to you with much love and joy and you seem to be at peace with this. Never doubt your gifts. We love you and want you to know this to be true.

*Journal exercise:*

What words did the angels give you today? Think about it and journal about it.

# August 5

Children, be at peace for all is well. Listen to the whispers in your mind to keep you grounded. Do not be afraid to speak your truth and to be your own person. Life is good for we will help you through the difficult times. Let the goodness of your heart shine for all you see today. Let the light that you are be shown to all you meet.

## Journal exercise:

How did your light shine for someone you met today? Think about it and journal about it.

# August 6

Create a new way of thinking that brings in more positive energy for you. Let this energy bring you to new places in your life. It is up to you where you want to go, for you are the co-creator in your life and the Universe is there to help you. The Universe will help you to keep up the momentum of positive thinking and living. Continue to make the effort to be positive and see where it brings you. Sometimes, your thinking gets a bit confused about what will make you happy. Your direction could bring you harm if pursued. We, your angels, are speaking of addictions and dare-devil activities that some people are attracted to. We suggest looking below the momentary feeling of ecstasy and seeing what is driving these activities. Where have they brought you to? Do two minutes of ecstasy bring you happiness or loathing of self? Do you feel at peace and feel your angels around you? Or do you feel like you shouldn't be doing this because it only brings on more depression and self-loathing? Talk to us, children. We want to help you. Ask us for help, for we are here for you. We send you Angel Blessings on this wonderful day.

## Journal exercise:

Is there something you did that you thought would make you feel good but instead brought on self-loathing? Think about it and journal about it.

# August 7

*Dear Children,*

We ask you today to consider those who are suffering so much in your world. Consider the pain that others are going through. The daily hunger pains, the daily fears of danger. We ask you to send healing light to all parts of the world, and to ask that the angels be there at this trying time. God is with all who are suffering and feels a lot of love for them. Know that the more light placed in all regions of the world, the brighter they will become.

## Journal exercise:

How can you help today to send the light of love to all parts of the world? Think about it and journal about it.

# August 8

## Dear Children,

We, your angels, are here to tell you that we are with you during these interesting times on the Earth plane. It may not seem like we are here for you, but we truly are. We know this is the time you need us the most. There are more people on the Earth plane who are becoming interested in who and what we are. We are working behind the scenes and working to help the light workers to help those on the Earth plane. We are giving help with the changes that are to come and helping with the transitions that are taking place. Ask us for help, don't be afraid, and also know we will not leave you.

## Journal exercise:

Do you feel that this is a time in your life when you need your angels more than before? Think about it and journal about it.

# August 9

*Dear Children,*

Each day you learn lessons by which to live life. What is your lesson for today? Do you feel that when you go through something difficult there is a lesson to be learned? Or do you turn to anger, loathing, and acting out? Do you let your ego run you ragged with negative self-talk, and take the incident so personally that it paralyses you from moving on? Or do you sit back and look at the situation from both sides with compassion and understanding of where everyone is coming from? It really is your choice to look at the situation from a negative view point, or try to find the good in what has happened. When you make the choice to be positive, you will notice a difference in how you feel about the situation. How you deal with this is for you only to decide. When you feel your heart's love, and the brightness of your light shining, you will have found happiness. We all want to feel genuinely happy, and this can truly happen. Just let the light shine in your heart, and sing out with joy. Feeling free from negative feelings is the right choice. Celebrate your happiness and love. Celebrate the freedom from negative thoughts. Celebrate today!

## Journal exercise:

How are you going to let the light shine on you today and celebrate the great day that it is? Think about it and journal about it.

# August 10

*Dear Children,*

Let your fears dissipate from your heart. Let your concerns fade away. Know that we care, and will help you to feel at peace at all times. Know that we are near, and will help you to understand the truth of the situation. Listen to your core truth of who you are and be clear of what this truth is.

Stay with your truth and don't be afraid to tell what you're all about.

*Journal exercise:*

What is your truth today? Think about it and journal about it.

# August 11

*Dear Children,*

What is the greatest gift you can give yourself? We, your angels, want to let you know it's not something that you can buy from a store or online website. It is something that can grow when cared for, yet it's not a plant. Do know what this gift is? We are talking about the gift of self-care and making sure this is an important part of your daily life. As aspects of daily self-care, eating food that is good for you is important, taking the right vitamins, and getting outside into the fresh air. You also receive this gift when you are around people who are caring toward you, whether it is family, friends or coworkers. Self-care is sometimes forgotten because you often take care of others more than you take care of yourself. We ask you to be more mindful of this and to see how you can take better care of yourself. We want you to know how much we love you and how important self-care is for all of you on the Earth plane.

*Journal exercise:*

How do you experience the gift of self-care in your life? What can you do to make improvements in your self-care? Think about it and journal about it.

# August 12

We, your angels, want you to know that looking to the angels for inspiration will help you to share your ideas in many creative ways. We will help you to express all that is within your heart. When asking us for this inspiration, know that we are with you. Your inspiration can come in the form of writing, poetry, song, painting or dance. Imagine the angels are with you, through every step of the creative process that you have decided to take part in.

## Journal exercise:

Ask the angels for inspiration in some form of creative expression. Think about it and journal about it.

# *August 13*

Listen to the sound of the environment around you. Is it noisy? Is it quiet? Listen to the sounds within you. Are they happy, are they sad; is your voice loud, or is it soft? When you listen to the sounds around you and the sounds within, it helps you to feel centered and mindful of all that is happening. Let go of the sounds on the outside and listen within. What are you hearing? What are you feeling and knowing? Go deeper within, underneath the negative feelings, and feel the peace and light and love. Feel the goodness and know that you are loved always.

## *Journal exercise:*

Sit for a few minutes and listen to the sounds around you. What are you hearing? What are you feeling? Think about it and journal about it.

# August 14

*Dear Angels,*

What message do you have for us today?

## Dear Children,

We want you to know that we are around when you look at the clouds in the sky. Sometimes there may be a shape of an angel or some other symbol, such as a feather. We are showing you we are there for you, at that very moment. Look for clouds near the sun at the end of the day, just before the sun goes down below the horizon. See if you can find the shape of some sort of angel. You can also ask to receive a sign that the angels are around by looking at the sky, among the cloud formations. Find a large space on a partly cloudy day and look up at the sky. What angelic shapes and forms do you see? Have fun and invite family or friends to join you. We wish you many angel blessings today.

## Journal exercise:

Go to the beach, a field or to the top of a hill and watch the clouds on a partly-cloudy day. What formations did you find in the clouds? Think about it and journal about it.

# August 15

Balancing your life with good food, good friends and abundance is all you really need in order to be happy. Knowing that you have these things can help you to have peace in your life and clarity about what is important to you. Of course, there are more things that can be put into the equation for happiness, but start with these three for now.

## Journal exercise:

What things in your life make you happy at this time? Think about it and journal about it.

# August 16

When times get difficult, know that we, your angels, are here for you. Know that we will not leave you no matter what. Listen to the silence deep within your heart, not what your head is saying to you. Your head speaks from the ego and your heart speaks of the light and love that you are. Try to remember this when times get difficult for you. When you listen with your heart, you will also hear your angels speak to you.

## Journal exercise:

What is your heart saying to you at this moment? Think about it and journal about it.

## August 17

Today we sing of our love and of all our Creator has done for us. It is a song of peace and calmness. Thank you, dear God, for your love and the peace you bring to so many. We thank you for the beauty that is there for all to see and we thank you for the bounty of all that we have. We are grateful for all that you do for us and we thank you for all that you are.

## Journal exercise:

What are you grateful for today? Think about it and journal about it.

# August 18

## Dear Children,

We thank you for all that you have done to help others on the Earth plane. We ask that you do not forget to help yourself also. We are speaking of being a receiver and not a giver. We are concerned for you because we feel you need to be able to receive. We also feel that some boundaries need to be made by you so that you can have time to yourself. We ask you to think about this and come up with a plan for yourself. Light workers are so susceptible to not making time for themselves. How can they help others and not take care of themselves? Please think about this.

## Journal exercise:

How are you taking care of yourself today? Think about it and journal about it.

# August 19

*Dear Children,*

We, your angels, have a message for you today from a collective of your angels. As we stand here behind you with our hands upon your shoulders, know that much healing is being sent to you on this day. Since we are a group of angels who are with you, know that our love for you is boundless. We always send out love to those who ask for it. You can ask for this healing love at any time, day or night. We, your angels, ask you to sit here quietly and enjoy the love that is being sent to you at this time.

## *Journal Exercise:*

Sit in your chair for a few minutes and feel the angels close to you, sending you love. How does it feel? Think about it and journal about it.

# August 20

Go to the depths of your being and be at peace, for today is a new day. We say this because it is a day when your life could change dramatically. We are not saying this is definite, but a possibility. Who have you met today? Whom have you spoken to? What did you read or hear today? Each day is a new day, so embrace it and enjoy what transpires for you. We feel that sometimes you are not embracing each day as a new opportunity. Let the sun shine in and let your curious nature help you to explore new opportunities.

## Journal exercise:

What has happened today that has helped you on your life path? Think about it and journal about it.

# August 21

## Dear Children of the Earth plane,

This is a time to be excited about all that is happening in the world. The veil is getting smaller and the Spirit world and the Earth plane are coming closer together. Communication and cooperation between the worlds is easier at this time. We want to remind you that we are always here for you. We pray for you to feel the peace we share with your world at this time. Letting go of differences and seeing the common bonds each of you have is more important at this time. We ask that you focus on the commonality of all beings. Doing this will help you to get to the heart place more easily than focusing only on the differences. We have always said that all are one and we mean this. We need you to understand this, so that peace will come to the Earth. We watch over all of you and we send you signs that we are doing so. We want you to feel our love daily and we want you to know that it will never wane.

What can you do to help with this process? The main thing you can do is to let go of the negative and embrace the positive, and accept others as they are. Then there will be no need for wars or weapons. There will be no need for children to be hungry or to suffer. We are all children of God and we are all loved by God. Embrace this and you will feel the pulse of the world in a time of complete peace.

## Journal exercise:

How do you feel about the changes that are happening on the Earth plane? Do you feel that your angels have become closer to you at this time? Think about it and journal about it.

# August 22

## Dear Children,

We are pleased that more people have more self-awareness. For some it has taken a long time to understand exactly who they are. For others it took less time. We mention this because you are all developing at your own pace and learning about who you are at the pace the Universe feels you can handle. Of course, many of you say, "I am not developing fast enough!" We say to keep your eye on all parts of the journey whether the progress is fast or slow. Know that each part is important. You may not see this at first but you will in time. So treasure your experiences, whether positive or negative, and know we are helping you along the way.

## Journal exercise:

The Universe is constantly asking us for patience in our journey. How can you enjoy your journey today? Think about it and journal about it.

# August 23

*Dear Children,*

Listening to your heart and knowing what you are feeling there will help you to be in your heart place. Feel the peace and clarity that is there. Do not be afraid of all that is occurring. We know you feel the energies that are being felt by so many on the Earth plane. Taking care of yourself will help you to remain grounded.

*Journal exercise:*

What are you feeling today? Think about it and journal about it.

# August 24

*Dear Angels,*

What message do you have for us today?

What do you want to ask us today? Talk to us so that we may answer back to you in plain language. Please understand that we are truly with you when you are speaking to us.

## Journal exercise:

What did ask your angels today? Did you receive a message from them in return? Think about it and journal about it.

# August 25

*Dear Children,*

We, your angels, want you to know that asking for help from the angels and all in the Universe is not a sign of weakness. When you ask for assistance it is truly a sign of strength. Please feel free to speak about this with us.

## *Journal exercise:*

What do you want help with today from the Universe? Think about it and journal about it.

# August 26

*Dear Angels,*

What message do you have for us today?

We want to wish you Angel Blessings and that this day brings you many blessing in a big way or in a small way. Share your light and brightness to all whom you meet, today. Share with them a story about your angels and how they have helped you in your life. Let your story be full of joy.

## Journal exercise:

What sort of blessings did you receive today, as you went through your day? Think about it and journal about it.

# *August 27*

*Dear Angels,*

What information do you have for us today?

We bring you joyful greetings of the day. We ask you to be at peace and know that we are here for you. Blessed are those who find the peace within themselves. We thank you for your ability to stay patient with all that is happening at this time. We thank you greatly for helping all those in need.

## *Journal exercise:*

What do you need to be patient about today? Think about it and journal about it.

# August 28

Live your life in faith that you are supported by the Universe. Know that the angels are with you every step of the way. Be patient with the journey, for it may not go in the way you think it should. Ask for God's blessing in all that you do. Let the love in your heart be the catalyst for keeping your journey alive and well.

Embrace both the good times and the difficult times as you go on with your journey, for both are part of what you need to experience.

## Journal exercise:

What is difficult for you at this time? Think about it and journal about it.

# August 29

*Dear Angels,*

What message do you have for us today?

We say this to you today with much pleasure. Did you know that you are loved and that the Universe cares so much for you? We are so proud of how well you have dealt with all you have been given in your life. The path has been very difficult and you have fared so well. You are a survivor and you are a teacher. Let your peace and serenity be shown to all, and dwell in your heart place. Let your happiness show at all times.

## Journal exercise:

How are you feeling today and how will you show your joy to those around you? Think about it and journal about it.

## August 30

Reach deep into your heart to connect with your soul. When you can look to that place of comfort and peace then you will know that God is near and that your angels are around you always. Knowing that God is near, you can feel the pulse of His love and goodness. We are in such confusing places at times, yet we can feel the love of our angels and of God. Do not be afraid to go to that place where no harm can come to you.

## Journal exercise:

Do you feel the love of God and your angels today? Meditate and feel their love for you. Think about it and journal about it.

# August 31

*Dear Angels,*

What message do you have for us today concerning peaceful living?

We are glad you asked this question. The message we have for you is this: *just be*. Strive to feel peace in your heart and to embrace the love there. Do not be too quick to judge others. Just accept them as they are and embrace their individuality. Your angels and God are waiting for you to embrace their love for you. Accepting this love is the key to a happy life.

## *Journal exercise:*

How can you just be? Think about it and journal about it.

# Living in the Heart Place with Your Angels

# September Messages

# September 1

## Dear Angels,

What message do you have for us, today?

## Dear Children,

Listening to the messages of the angels is a choice that only you can make. Hearing all we have to say to you in so many different ways is very personal and individual too. You can ask your angels to give you a sign they are near you. How do your angels let you know they are near you? You can always ask them for guidance in this.

## Journal exercise:

What signs have your angels shown you they are near you? Think about it and journal about it.

# September 2

LOVE

L is for listening to the whispers of your angels deep in your heart.

O is for the orderly way the Angels guide you when you ask for help.

V is for the victory of never-ending peace in your heart when you hear the angels' messages.

E is for the extra-special guidance you receive when you ask for help from your healing angels.


## Journal exercise:

The angels encourage you to try doing an acronym for the word LOVE with your own meanings. Think about it and write the acronym in your journal.

# September 3

ANGEL

A Angels are always around you. They have messages for everyone who asks to receive an angel message.

N Noted for being at the right place at the right time.

G Glorious angels all around helping us get through our day.

E Eloquent messages we all receive from the angels, with much love.

L Loving angels helping the world to heal and to be at peace.


## Journal exercise:

Acronyms are fun to do. Try doing one for ANGELS. Think about it and write it in your journal.

# September 4

Always trust your first gut feeling on a decision that you need to make for yourself or others. You can sense your gut feeling deep within your heart where there is no room for ego to be. The peace that you feel from this decision lets you know it is right for you. The angels encourage you to feel at peace and to feel that all will be fine.

## Journal exercise:

Has there ever been a time when you made a decision from a gut feeling? How did it turn out? Were you happy with the decision that you made? Think about it and journal about it.

# September 5

*To Our Children,*

We ask that you consider the fact that we are here with you and will never leave you. We are always close to you and when you call on us, it is free. There is no payment expected. We only ask you to listen to us and keep the parts of the conversation that make sense to you. We are here with you always.

*Journal exercise:*

Is there something you want to ask your angels or talk about with them? Think about it and journal about it.

# September 6

Think of all that you have and all that you treasure. We, your angels, ask you to be at peace with this. We feel that sometimes you do not fully appreciate all that you have. Sometimes you think you need more and that you cannot live without this something more. However, we ask you to look a little deeper and ask yourself if possibly someone else could use what you feel you need at this particular time. Is there some way you can help someone else to get by day to day? What resources do you have to help that person or group of people? We feel that the more you help one another, the more meaningful your life will be in the end. We ask you to go deep into your heart and ask, "What would the angels like me to do when I see a person in need?" What you do does not have to be big. It can be a smile to that person; it can be buying a cup of coffee or giving them a resource that will truly help them. It can also be giving away things such as books, clothing or furniture to someone in need. We ask you to take a look at all that you possess and decide what you can do without that would benefit another person. We ask you to truly consider this. Thank you and angel blessings.

## Journal exercise:

What can you do today to help someone? Think about it and journal about it.

# September 7

Be at peace, for many blessings are bestowed on you during your lifetime. Let the joy you feel each day be a blessing in itself. The many blessings that you have can accumulate to great proportions and will outweigh the things that are not blessings in your life. Your angels will remind you of your blessings continually and put you in positions where you have to recognize them. In doing this you can choose to let your light shine brightly to all you see and speak to on a daily basis. Let your joy be noticeable and let your blessings accumulate.

## Journal exercise:

Today think of the blessings that you have in your life. In your journal write down each blessing and thank God and the angels for each one.

## September 8

Let your fears be dismissed when it comes to feeling there is scarcity. Keep your eye on the vision that you have for yourself and let the Universe help you with this. The Universe is helping you to reach this goal. When you keep your thoughts positive there is no room for negativity to come through.

### Journal exercise:

What fears do you have today about reaching your goals? Work out some ways to have only positive thoughts concerning your vision or goal. Think about it and journal about it.

## September 9

To write what you are grateful for in your life each day is a way of thanking the Universe for all you have been given in your life. No matter how small or how big, being grateful lets the Universe know you are thankful. Try making a list of 10 things you are grateful for each day. They can all be different or some can be the same. Feel the pleasure of the Universe as you give thanks. Giving thanks lets the Universe know that all is well in your world.

## Journal exercise:

Make a list of ten things you are grateful for today. Do this each day for a week. How does it feel? Think about it and journal about it.

## September 10

Who are the angels who help us with healing? There are several angels who help, but the angel who is most connected with healing is Archangel Raphael. He will help you with healing on a personal basis and also when you are helping others to heal. He helps with healing on all levels: physical, emotional, mental and spiritual.

### Journal exercise:

What healing do you want Archangel Raphael help you with? How has he helped you with healing in the past? Think about it and journal about it.

# September 11

When life is too busy, go to the heart place where love and peace exist. Know that your angels are with you and they love you very much. Angels are helping you to cope with the issues in your life and helping to bring you peace. Know that the heart place is a place where clarity and serenity exist at all times and thank the Universe for all that has been given to you.

## Journal exercise:

Put on some music and light a candle. Ask the angels to help you find the heart place that is within you. Listen to their words. What do they say to you? Think about it and journal about it.

# September 12

Let the love in your heart reach out to all who are in need of some love today. Let the peace that you feel spread to all who need to feel peace. Let the clarity of all that you know be a help to you and to all who you see today. Know that the angels love you and know that they are messengers of love and guidance.

## Journal exercise:

How do you feel today? Do you feel that the love in your heart can reach out to all whom you meet? Think about it and journal about it.

# September 13

We thank you for your perseverance and willingness to continue on your road. You may take some turns on your path, but they will bring you to enrichment and increased blessings. You have free will in the choice of following your true path. Everyone comes to forks in the road, which one you take is up to you. We thank you, dear children, for exploring new avenues. We thank you for believing in us as we believe in you. We are always here for you and all you have to do is ask for guidance.

## Journal exercise:

Have you ever had a time in your life when you have had the choice of two roads? Which path did you take? Were you happy with the choice? Did the new path help you manifest the vision you had for yourself? Think about it and journal about it.

# September 14

When the angels gather around you, they sing their songs of joy and love. They will always be with you. Blessed are those who feel the love of the angels and their peace. The angels have a lot of room in their hearts for you. They will not leave you in any way. They promise you this. The angels love to sing songs of peace and of love. Ask your angels for guidance at any time. Angel Blessings to all.


## Journal exercise:

What guidance have you had from the angels lately? Did you feel their presence around you? How did it feel to you? Think about it and journal about it.

## September 15

Angel feathers remind us that our angels are around us at all times. The feathers always seem to be around at the time we need to hear from our angels. It's so comforting to know they are around us. Archangel Michael and Archangel Raphael explain about having a feather appear at the exact time we need to hear from them, "We are always here for you and there are always signs that we are around. It is just that you have to notice them." Sometimes we are too busy to notice the different signs, sometimes we just do not think to see if there are signs of the angels around us. But they are there. Sometimes the signs are subtle and sometimes not. Be on the look-out for both and be at peace in your heart knowing that the angels are with you always.

### Journal exercise:

Have feathers appeared at the exact time you needed to know that the angels were around you? Think about it and journal about it.

# September 16

Today you will shine your light on all whom you meet. Shine your light on those in the dark, and who do not know about the light in their own hearts. Be at peace, for your light truly shines brightly to all. Ask your angels to help you to stay in a place where pure intention is constant. Staying calm at all times can help with the clarity of all that is happening.

## Journal exercise:

What can you do today to shine your light for others? Think about it and journal about it.

# September 17

Angels are around us, protecting us in every way. Open your eyes to all that the angels do for you on a particular day. Angels protect us and our space and they help us to heal our bodies and our emotions. They give us messages of love and they help us to appreciate one another. They are full of love and help us to feel at peace. The angels will never give us a message that is upsetting or painful to us in any way. They help us create our dreams and put just the right people in our space to help us on our way. The angels help us to keep our space clear when we ask for their help. We each have a guardian angel who is with us always. The angels will not forget us but they will not force themselves on us. They will put little thoughts into our minds to help us on our daily journey.

## Journal exercise:

What message have the angels given to you recently? Think about it and journal about it.

# September 18

Angels whisper in our ear. Tell us a message, make it clear.

We hear messages of love always; they are never messages of fear. Our angels love us and want us to know that they care.

## Journal exercise:

When hearing messages from your angels, what do they tell you? Think about it and journal about it.

## September 19

Imagine dancing with the angels throughout the day, dancing to the perfect music and living your life in harmony and clarity. It's as if music has been written to accompany the outcomes of what is happening. The angels in their choirs sing beautiful music as they help guide you in your life. It's as if you are floating through your life effortlessly, dancing to the tune of joy and happiness and peace.

### Journal exercise:

Imagine dancing with the angels. Think about what music you are dancing to and how many angels are with you. Write about this in descriptive language in your journal.

# September 20

Dreams beyond your imagination can happen when you are aware of your angels and how they guide you on your path. The angels will do all they can to help your dreams come true. They pay attention to your intentions and the amount of love you have in this endeavor. They will put people into your path and they will help the journey to be a bit easier. You are walking your path now because you are alive and aware of what can happen.

It's not a matter of getting to your path. You are on your path now. Don't forget this…Enjoy the ride and know that you doing well…. Think of where you started and where you are going. What do you know now that you didn't know before? Who have you met who has helped you so far? What are you learning now that you were not aware of before? In dealing with people or situations in your life, what has helped you to see the good when you might have had a negative feeling or opinion about them?

## Journal exercise:

How do you think you are doing on your path at this time? Have you received a new direction or more information that will help you on your way? Think about it and journal about it.

## September 21

When angels are near and speaking quietly to you, know that they have only positive things to say. Know that the angels are guiding you on your path, showing you their presence by little synchronicities. The angels are helpers of God. He guides them to do what is needed to help you in your life. When you think of your path in retrospect, you will see the perfect orchestration of your life's journey.

## Journal exercise:

What synchronicities have you noticed in your life lately? Think about it and journal about it.

## September 22

*Dear Angels,*

What do you have to say to us today? What is your message?

We want to keep reminding you of the light that is in your heart space. That space is where you are at peace and where you can feel the presence of a loving God. The heart space is where calm and clarity live, as well as serenity, trust and integrity. This special place is the essence of who you are. The angels are there too and they help you to know this through their guidance and love. When life is stressful or you are sad or just become so busy you can hardly function, go to this heart space and know that all is well with you. It may be easier to find this heart space in a quiet room listening to soft music. Being with God and the angels in your heart space is where you will experience peace. When you go there, your walls fall down, your anger dissolves and you are peaceful and calm, because you know your angels and God are there for you.

## Journal exercise:

Try going to your heart space and experiencing the peace and the calm. What do you feel? What do you hear? What do you see? Think about it and journal about it.

# September 23

We pray each day that you will know the vision you have for yourself. We ask God for His healing when you ask us, your angels, for healing. It's like double insurance that God hears you. We ask His light to shine upon you and to brighten your hearts so you can feel the love of God's presence. Please do not continue to ask when is this going to happen. You are already on your way to being who you are meant to be. It's a matter of trust and a matter of pure intention to achieve your vision. When life is lived to its fullest your light is shining bright and you feel love in your heart.

## Journal exercise:

Do you feel the love of God's light in your heart? Think about it and journal about it.

# September 24

*Dear Angels,*

What message do you have for us today?

Today's word is PEACE.

P Prepare for the seasonal changes that will be taking place soon.

E Examine the priorities that you have undertaken and work on them individually.

A Abundance comes in many forms.

C Create a place for meditation in your home, a place you can call your own.

E Entertain the thought that with love we find peace in our hearts and in our world.

*Journal exercise:*

Try writing your own acronym for PEACE. Think about it and write it in your journal.

# September 25

*Dear Angels,*

What message do you have for us today?

Light workers, we ask that you help those who are in fear. We ask that you help them to safety if safety is needed. We will help you in helping them. Ask for our help and together we can be even more effective.

## Journal exercise:

Are you a seeker or a light worker? Think about it and journal about it.

# September 26

Speaking of your beliefs to those who share the same views can be very rewarding for everyone concerned. Have you ever thought about speaking about who the angels are and how they have helped you? Don't be afraid to talk about your angels. By sharing your experiences, you help others to be aware of their angels. You may not know that you are helping, but know that you are meant to speak about us. We are not a big secret, most people have heard of us. There are people who don't know how the angels can help them personally. When you share your personal experiences with others, this will help them to understand who the angels are and what they do.

## Journal exercise:

What stories can you share about the angels with the people in your life? Think about it and journal about it.

# September 27

*Dear Angels,*

What message do you have for us today?

*Dear Children,*

We ask that you not waste the resources of your planet. We ask that you value each resource as a precious gift from God and the Universe. We are concerned with the horrific things happening because of the lack of regard for these gifts. Precious resources in nature have been overused, and some animals and plants have become extinct. We ask you to take note of this and to be mindful of the resources you use. The Earth needs to heal and it will do just that. It is suffering, but it is also reviving. Help empower each other to show your love towards one another and to see the beauty in the world we live in. We can then survive the changes taking place and live in peace.

*Journal exercise:*

What do you feel about the state of the world at this time? How can you do your part to help the world revive back to its healthy self? Think about it and journal about it.

# September 28

What message do you have for us today?

Focus on what is right for you at this time. Be an individual in this matter and do what is good for you. Today so many people only focus on the accepted way to approach a situation. It is okay to hear a different drummer. It seems to us, your angels, that we can help you with this. It's time to be who you really are, not just who you think you are. Ask us for help with this. By focusing on the positive you will always succeed.

## Journal exercise:

Are you having difficulty deciding on the right way to solve a particular issue? Do you want to walk on the path that everyone perceives as being the right way to solve it or do you have your own opinion which is different from what others may think? Think about it and journal about it.

# September 29

*Dear Angels,*

What message do you have for us today?

Children, do you not believe us when we tell you that you can ask for help from the Universe? We ask this because there are so many people who do not know that they can. Don't be afraid to tell the masses that they, also, can ask for help from the Universe. We know there are many people who are very afraid of doing this. The manifesting powers of the Universe are open to all and when your intentions are pure and positive the Universe is there to help you. The angels can help you tell others about this and guide you to where this message is needed. Spreading the word that God and our angels are always around us will help a great deal. This news will bring much comfort to those who doubt.

## *Journal exercise:*

How can you spread the word about the existence of angels and their love for us? Think about it and journal about it.

# September 30

*Dear Angels,*

What information do you want to give to us today?

The essence of someone's aura truly tells you where they have been. It tells you how they are feeling emotionally and what baggage is with them at a particular time. Everyone has an aura which shows this information. It is like a blueprint of your state of mind at a particular time. We mention this because even though someone's aura isn't normally seen, it is felt by everyone. Have you ever been around a person who seems filled with negativity and resentment? All you want to do is to get away from them. You find you are feeling a bit sick and you feel that you really need to leave. You are feeling their aura. We suggest that when this happens you ground and protect yourself. There are many methods to do this. You can imagine yourself in a bubble of light that is protecting you from all harm. You can also imagine roots growing out the soles of your feet and the roots going deep down into the ground where they are anchored by large rocks.

This is a difficult time and many people are feeling stressed, upset and confused. Running into these types of energies is very possible at anytime. Protecting yourself is very important. Another way of protecting yourself is to be sure you have some outside time and connection with nature. We know you know most of this information, but we are gently reminding you of this to keep you aware of what is happening at this time.

## Journal exercise:

What are some ways you can ground and protect when you meet a person with negative energy? Think about it and journal about it.

# Living in the Heart Place with Your Angels

# October Messages

# October 1

*Dear Angels,*

What message do you have for us today?

Place your hand over your heart; this is where your heart place is. This is the place you go to when you seek peace and love. This is the place where you connect with your angels and your God. It is a place of serenity and goodness, with no room for negativity. This heart place has no room for anger and self-loathing. Purity of heart is all that is needed. So many people do not realize this heart place does indeed exist, because they were never told of its existence. Can you imagine not knowing of this heart place? Today go out to tell at least one person about the heart place. When we are doing this we help one more person to see where their heart space is. We will be done when the entire world knows about the heart place and there is no more fighting anywhere in the world. Peace in our hearts means world peace. Then there will be no need for war.

## *Journal exercise:*

Just think if everyone knew where their heart place was, there would be peace in our world. How can you help others to find their heart place? Think about it and journal about it.

# October 2

The ability to co-create is something that we are all given by the Universe. So many of us do not realize this is possible. By co-creation, we, the angels, mean that you are able to help in manifesting your dreams in the way you would like. Asking the Universe for its light and its help makes the collaboration possible; co-creation keeps the work equal in manifesting. What this means is that you can ask the Universe for help, and it will give it, but you must do your part as well, you must take the actions necessary to make things happen. Working from your heart place, you will know what to do and how proceed with co-creation. When you ask the Universe for what you want, then do the footwork, the Universe works with you to make it a perfect creation. Therefore do not be afraid to ask the Universe for help. The angels, your guides and loved ones, and God want this to happen for you. Trust and all will be well.

*Journal exercise:*

How are you letting the Universe be a partner in co-creating your reality? Think about it and journal about it.

# October 3

*Dear Angels,*

What message do you have for us on love?

Our message to you is to embrace the love that is in your heart space. Let this love grow, be nurtured and taken care of. Love is the feeling of overwhelming happiness. It is a feeling of knowing you are cared for and very treasured by the people who are important in your life. Love grows when light is shining in your heart space. There is a never-ending love deep in your heart. Along with the love you can feel the peace and calmness that is there. Think of pinks, whites and greens swirling in your heart place, keeping the love safe and permanent. Feel the good feeling and know that love is always there for you.

*Journal exercise:*

How is love present in your life today? Think of three examples of love that is present in your life. Think about it and journal about it.

# October 4

*Dear Angels,*

What message do you have for us today?

*Dear Children,*

We would like to take the time to say that we are always here for you and that you can ask us anything at anytime. We always hear your requests and we will help you by putting the necessary people, places and things in your path. We suggest that you enjoy all that you experience so that you can find the joy of your life's journey. Many people don't understand this, so we are helping you to understand it.

*Journal exercise:*

What people, places or things have you noticed lately being put into your path that can help you in some way? Think about it and journal about it.

# October 5

Listen to you heart and to what it is saying to you at this time. When you listen to your heart, you know that this is where peace and serenity reside. The angels help you to find your heart place. God helps you to find this place of peace too. So many of us think with only our heads and do not consider our hearts. The angels ask us to consider thinking with our hearts. Why do they say this? Your heart is not only where peace and serenity reside, but also where hope, love and calm are. The angels know that to think with your heart is not always possible, but considering the heart when making decisions or dealing with difficult situations helps a lot. The state of the world needs more heart-place thinking and they hope you start to think from there.

## Journal exercise:

How can you start to think from the heart place? Think about it and journal about it.

# October 6

*Dear Angels,*

What message do you have for us today?

*Dear Children,*

We are here to say that there is no choice but to go with the flow. Going with the flow means living your life in a calm way. We ask you: what good does it do to live in a way that is full of anxiety or upset? It truly gets you nowhere. Live in your heart space: thinking of your angels and of your Higher Power helps. Prayer helps also. Singing and music help you to go get to your heart place. Meditation helps you get there, as well. There truly are many ways to get to the heart place.

*Journal exercise:*

How will you get to your heart place today? Think about it and journal about it.

# October 7

You need to be able to sit down, meditate, and know that deep in your heart is where peace and serenity lie. You can do this often and take comfort in the rituals that you engage in. Know that the heart place is where positive thinking lives. Your angels reside there, as well. You can get to your center through music and through positive affirmations. The angels feel you know this and are reminding you so that you can help others to find the heart place too.

## Journal exercise:

What is your ritual or routine for getting to your heart place? Think about it and journal about it.

# October 8

The angels are here as you sit down to meditate and ask for a message today. In meditation, you see that their whispers are present. When you get to your heart place, you can hear their voices speaking to you. Opening the heart place allows your light to shine to all you know. The brightness can help many people in their difficult times. The angels are with you and showing you what needs to be done at all times. As light workers, you are directed to those who need some direction or guidance in their lives. Speaking from personal experience can help those who have questions and want some direct answers. Do not be afraid to tell your story, for when you tell it you help others who may be in the place you were in the past.

## Journal exercise:

What is a story that you think would be helpful for others to hear? Think about it and journal about it.

# October 9

*Dear Angels,*

What message do you have for us today?

*Dear Children,*

We guide you to the place where love resides. We take you to a place of peace and serenity. We want you to know that our love is always there for you, never leaving you. We will guide you and help you to hear the music of your heart. Everyone has music in his or her heart. Can you hear your heart music?

*Journal exercise:*

Can you hear the music in your heart? Do you need to ask the angels for help with this? Think about it and journal about it.

# October 10

*Dear Children,*

We are with you everyday to help with your concerns and assure you that all will be fine. We ask you to trust that we, your angels, will help you and help the sequence of events to fall into place the way it is meant to. Sometimes you want to make the process go faster, you look at your time schedule and things don't seem to be falling into place. This can be maddening. We remind you that everything happens in divine timing, not on your time schedule. Again, we ask you to trust the process and timing that the Universe has for you. It's truly paramount for your inner peace. Ask us, your angels, to help with this guidance. We will help anytime when you ask us.

## *Journal exercise:*

Have you asked your angels for help today? Do you understand what divine timing means? Think about it and journal about it.

# October 11

Let the peace in your hearts help you to cope with everyday concerns. Go to your heart place deep within you where there is calm and clarity. We, your angels, thank you for all that has been asked of us, for we are glad to help you. We will not disappoint you nor will we ignore your requests. We want you to know that your God is our God. We are merely God's helpers and the ones to show you the way to your God's love for all of you. We will help you to understand the path that you have been walking on and will help you to feel peace in all that is happening. Don't be afraid, we are here and we will guide you for all time.

## Journal exercise:

What can you ask the angels to help you with today? Think about it and journal about it.

# October 12

## Dear Children,

Creativity is something that happens in stages. There is the planning that goes with the visualization of the project. Then there is the planning of materials and how you will execute the start of the project. Then there is the actual creation of the project.

Life is like that too. We are co-creators with the Universe concerning our lives. We visualize our vision for ourselves and then the Universe helps us to work towards the goal by putting people, places and things in our path. However, we only have partial control over how our vision manifests. We work towards our goal and it is created in divine timing, not in the timing we visualize it to be.

## Journal exercise:

What project are you working on and how are all the pieces coming together? Think about it and journal about it.

# October 13

Shine your light on all that you do. Be confident in your life's goals. Know that you can reach the highest rung on the highest level. Strive to be the best in all that you do. The angels are with you. They will always be there for you. Know this and be at peace.

## Journal exercise:

What are you striving for today in which you want to be the best in every way? Think about it and journal about it.

# October 14

Let go of your fears. Know that there are so many possibilities for positive outcomes. Never let the fears lead you. Work past them and move into brighter places where your joy and peace live. When you feel passion and joy, you know that your dream is right for you. Let your passion be the driver of your life. Let the love in your heart flow into all that you are. God and the angels love us and they help us to travel the path we have chosen in our lifetime. You are you and no one else. Do not be afraid to be who you are. The light at your core shines brightly. It starts in your heart and shows with your smile.

## Journal exercise:

How can you help your fears go into the background and your passion come to the forefront of your heart? Think about the passion you feel and then journal about it.

# October 15

Go to ends of the earth to find your passion. Figure out what you are passionate about and how you want to manifest it. Ask your angels for guidance and to help you find the path you need that will make your passion work for you.

## Journal exercise:

What passion do you have that is in need of goal setting? Think about it and ask your angels to help you journal about it.

## October 16

Today write to your angels about what you feel in your heart. Write them a letter and ask them some questions that you have concerns about. You will find this a very interesting exercise. What information did you get in writing this letter? Then write a letter that is the angels' answer to you. What additional information did you get in this exercise? Did you enjoy doing this and hearing from your angels?

### Journal exercise:

Write the letters and journal about your experience.

# October 17

The angels are asking you to write what you are hearing about the word *love*. Be still and be at peace, then ask the angels to talk to you about love. What do you hear the angels say? Write down everything that you hear.

## Journal exercise:

Ask the angels to talk to you about love. Listen and journal about it.

# October 18

Go into your heart place and feel the warmth of the healing love there, immerse yourself with its peace. God and the angels are there with you, and love you unconditionally. They are there to keep you safe and to show you the love waiting to keep you peaceful. You will gain clarity about all that life has brought to you. Let the peace of your heart draw you into the love that is there.

## Journal exercise:

Today go into your heart place and be at peace. How does it feel? What thoughts come to mind when you are there? Think about it and journal about it.

# October 19

Walking the path of peace and love can lead to much happiness. When on this path you will find the quiet deep within. Listen to the gentle whispers of your angels and the Universe. Thank you, dear angels, for all that you do. Thank you to the Source of All for helping to find this heart place and for being there.

*Journal exercise:*

How thankful are you today? Write a prayer of thanks to the Universe in your journal.

# October 20

*Dear Children,*

Today we, your angels, share with you this meditation.

Imagine that we, your angels, are dancing and singing songs of joy all around you. Hear the magical melodies and the words of our songs. We have so much love for you and we tell you of our wishes for you. Let the joy in all that you hear from us be a magical experience. We will continue to communicate many messages of love, hope and clarity to you.

## Journal exercise:

What were the angels saying to you as you did this meditation? Think about it and journal about it.

# October 21

*Dear Angels,*

What message do you have for us today?

The message for today is to know that when you are in your heart space peace and love reign there. The love there is the love that you give to all as you live each day. Protect your heart place by surrounding it with light. Your angels are there and they help you to see the depth to which the love goes. You can show your love by singing out with joy, or writing about it in a journal, or saying a kind word to someone who crosses your path. We ask you to share what is in your heart place with others you meet.

*Journal exercise:*

What can do you to show your love for others today? Think about it and journal about it.

# October 22

Come to the heart place where you are safe and loved. Only good things come from the heart place. The angels live there too. They will fill your heart with even more love. In your heart place the feelings of goodness and peace keep you safe at all times.

## Journal exercise:

How do you feel when you are in your heart place? Think about it and journal about it.

## October 23

Let the angel whispers be heard deep within your heart place. When listening to their words know deep within you the love they have for you. Be at peace, dear children, the angels are near you at all times. Let childlike banter be a part of who you are. Having fun with your friends and family lets your light shine today and always. A sense of humor is good to have, for laughter with all whom you meet is a good way to remain young and free.

## Journal exercise:

What did you laugh about today? Think about it and then journal about it.

## October 24

The angels ask that today you take notice of the changes that are happening outside. Leaves are falling and continuing to change color. The flowers are fading and the harvest is brought in for storage for the winter. The birds are flying south and temperatures are turning colder. The long sleep of winter will soon be upon us.

### Journal exercise:

How are you preparing for the seasonal changes? Think about it and journal about it.

# October 25

*Dear Angels,*

What message do you have for us today?

We encourage you to write a letter to your guardian angel. Don't be afraid to write what is on your mind. Write from the heart. Let your angel help you formulate what is truly on your mind. Then write a letter that is the angel's answer to you.

## *Journal exercise:*

Go into your heart place and write a letter to your guardian angel. Then write what your angel replies.

# October 26

*Dear Children,*

We thank you for your letter and we pray that you liked our message back to you. We encourage writing to your archangel of choice, asking for help with an issue. Write the letter and then the reply from the archangel. Know that your archangels are always with you and know they want to help you in any way possible.

## *Journal exercise:*

Think about which archangel you want to write to and write the letter. Then write a reply from the archangel.

# October 27

*Dear Angels,*

What message do you have for us today?

Let your hopes, dreams and adventures be all that you want them to be. Please ask for help and we will help you on your journey at any time. Life is what you make it and you need to know that when you have lemons make lemonade. Focus on what is positive in your life and ask the Angels take care of the negative. Trust that they will help you with this.

## *Journal exercise:*

What would you like to ask the angels today to help you with? Think about it and journal about it.

# October 28

Angels help us understand what love is and how full of love our beings are. Do not forget the peace and serenity that is at hand. It is yours for the asking at all times. Listen deep within your heart and believe that the messages of love are from your angels and from our Source, who is God. They work together to help you on your path. Please don't worry about how your journey is going, as it is divinely led and all activity is occurring with divine timing.

## Journal exercise:

What messages of love have you heard from your angels today? Think about it and journal about it.

# October 29

## Dear Angels,

What is your message for us today?

## Dear Children,

We encourage you to do research about angels. As you may know, there are many different angels for the many different needs that you have. There are many different books and information websites where you can learn more. We want you to find out all you can about us. Enjoy your searches in the many different places where there is information about us.

## Journal exercise:

What information did you find in your research about the different angels and archangels? Think about it and journal about it.

## October 30

Open your hearts to the possibilities of what your life can be now and for your future. Try not to look to the past, if that was too painful for you. Learn from the past and look for what today and your future can bring to you in a positive way.

## Journal exercise:

Ask you angels to help with looking at what life is bringing you now and in the future. Think about it and journal about it.

# October 31

## Dear Angels,

What do you have to say to us today?

## Dear Child,

Our message to you is that you are love. We say this because the more you hear this the more you understand it. As a Child of God you are able to feel love and peace and to share it with all you know. Let your light shine and let it spread, for God's love will carry you through the difficult times and the happy times. Angels are with you always for they are made of love.

## Journal exercise:

How can you spread your love to others? Think about it and journal about it.

# Living in the Heart Place with Your Angels

# November Messages

# November 1

## Dear Angels,

What message do you have for us today?

The music of the Universe is the music that you hear within your heart. Listen to its soft melody and feel the peace it brings you. Let this music help you dance to the tune of your own dance and visions for your life. The angels are near and God is too. God is the director and the angels are in the choir singing their lovely chants to all to hear. Alleluia, Alleluia, listen carefully for the messages from your angels. In hearing their songs you can then sing your own, and the angels will hear you.

## Journal exercise:

What angel songs do you hear today? Think about it and journal about it.

# November 2

*Dear Angels,*

What message do you have for us today?

Love is the key to happiness. Giving love and receiving love is what life is all about. Love is where your angels are and they guide you to love in so many ways. They are here to help with understanding love and giving love to others. We ask you to listen to the words of your angels, and to feel their love for you. Angels talk in whispers and they talk loudly too. They will talk to you in a way which you can understand. Open your hearts and minds to know how the angels speak to you. Be open to what they have to say. Feel the peace in your heart, know that the angels are speaking and listen to their messages. Their love is real and available to all.

## Journal exercise:

How have the angels helped you in the last few months? Have you felt their love throughout your days? Think about it and journal about it.

# November 3

*Dear Angels,*

What message do you have for us today?

We ask you to reach down deep in your heart to see what your heart is saying to you today. When you have done this you will know what we are saying, too, for we are in your heart. We give you much love and peace and clarity; we pray that you can feel all that we send you. When you are feeling down, or not at peace, go to your heart place and you will feel more at one with yourself and with the Universe.

*Journal exercise:*

Today find some quiet time, go to your heart place, and feel what your heart is saying to you. Think about it and journal about it.

# November 4

## Dear angels,

what do you have to say to the people reading this daily message? We say to you, happy day. Enjoy your day to the fullest. Let the love of your angels help you to have a fantastic day in every way. We celebrate, as you celebrate too. We dance and we sing. Let the Universe worry about things that are bothersome to you. Be at peace, and feel the clarity of what the Universe wants for you.

## Journal exercise:

Today, during your quiet time, imagine a celebration with the angels. It's just you and the angels. Write in great detail what your celebration is like…Who is there, what all of you do, which angels come to party with you. Think about it and journal about it. Try writing it as a meditation. Have fun.

# November 5

*Dear angels,*

What message do you have for us on this wonderful day?

We are here to say that patience is such a virtue. We know it is difficult for you, for you want things to happen at your specified time. Instead, be patient and live your life as if it was the first day of falling in love. Know that all is well, and that to live in the flow of life is living without expectations.

## *Journal exercise:*

What issues in your life are you feeling impatient about? How can the angels help you to go with the flow? Think about it and journal about it.

# November 6

*Dear Angels,*

What message do you have for us today?

We have many messages to give to you, but the main message is that we are here to help all of you. Our love is unconditional and everlasting. We come when we are asked for help and we guide you on your path throughout your life. It seems to us that you know about us, but are very hesitant about believing we can help you at times. This is normal, as this is what was taught to you during your lifetimes. We are closer now and we can help in so many ways. Don't hesitate to ask for help for we truly are with you. We do not take the place of God in any way, for we are God's messengers and work for him. He is our God, too.

## *Journal exercise:*

How does this help you to understand the path of the angels and why they are here for us at all times? Think about it and journal about it.

# November 7

## Dear Angels,

What messages do you have for us today?

What is your heart telling you today about how you can move beyond the obstacles that may be blocking you? How can we, your angels, help you with this? By asking for assistance you will receive the help you need. Let your heart bring you to a place of understanding and compassion and peace. Let your heart feel the clarity of the situation and the serenity that comes with it. We all have something that is troublesome at some point. Let your heart be your guide to enlightenment. Know that we, your angels, are with you today.

## Journal exercise:

Allow yourself to feel all that is within your heart. Be at peace and let the angels help you with your vision. Think about it and journal about it.

# November 8

Open you heart to all the blessings in your life today. Let the love you feel deep in your heart burst through and the feeling come to the forefront of your emotions. Let the angels help you to celebrate and feel this love. Ask for guidance with whatever you need, for they can help you.

## Journal exercise:

What blessings do you have today in your life? Think about it and journal about it.

# November 9

Celebrate today like you have never celebrated before. Let the message of love be for all you see in a day's time. Let peace and clarity be a reality for you at all times. Be in the heart place where peace resides and know that God and the angels are there too.

## Journal exercise:

Be in your heart place today and feel the peace that is there. How does this feel? Think about it and journal about it.

# November 10

*Dear Angels,*

What message do you have for us today?

Remember always that we love you, especially in times of difficulty. Let the sadness disperse and let a smile be given to you. Feel the joy in this feeling of love and know your angels and God are here with you today. When you are sad or angry you may find it hard to find the joy in your heart. However, joy is there when you go within and look for it. So go to that place of total joy and know you are not alone.

## *Journal exercise:*

How can you find joy when you are sad or angry? Think about it and journal about it.

# November 11

## Dear Archangel Michael,

What message would you like to give to us today?

## Dear Children,

Today, I would like to speak to you about personal safety. So many times you find yourself in a situation that may threaten your personal safety. I am here to remind you that when you call on me I am there with you, helping you to become safe once again. You can ask for protection when you travel by bus, train, or plane. Please be at peace and know that I am with you at all times.

Love,

Archangel Michael

## Journal exercise:

Write your own letter to Archangel Michael and ask him what message he has for you, then write down his answer to you.

# November 12

*Dear Angels,*

What message do you have for us on love in our world?

*Children,*

Know that love comes from the heart place, which we speak about so often. The heart place is deep within your core and only good and positive feelings are found there. You will find love, peace, serenity and clarity when you go there. What you won't find there is hate, anger, jealousy and sadness. The heart place for many is like a swirl of pinks and whites moving and mixing together, sometimes interspersing with different shades of green. It is where healing takes place. It is a place where you are happy and can always find joy. Let your heart rejoice and feel the healing of the love that is there.

Love is a precious gift. It is a gift you can give to yourself or it can be received from others. Enjoy the gift of love and savor it too. God and the angels are love and are in your heart place.

*Journal exercise:*

What is it like to be in your heart place? How do you feel when you are there? Think about it and journal about it.

# November 13

## Dear Angels,

What is your guidance for us today?

Today we want to speak about peace. It is always possible to feel peace in the world or to feel at peace with a decision we make. Then we can have the feeling of peace within us and around us. These are some affirmations you can use to help you feel peaceful:

☆ I feel at peace now in my heart center.

☆ I feel the angels near me and I feel their peace.

☆ I feel God with me and I am at peace.

☆ In peace we feel a satisfaction for all that is going on.

## Journal exercise:

Find you heart place where your peace is and stay there a few minutes, so you to can experience it. Think about and journal about it.

# November 14

Today we come to you with music and joy in our hearts. The music that we are hearing is music from the higher realms of the Universe. We, your angels, are so happy that you are now beginning to hear the messages that we send to you on a daily basis. You have been listening very intently and you do understand the messages given to you. As you know, our messages can come in so many different ways. Don't be afraid to ask us for guidance today. Listen closely for our messages, dear children.

## Journal exercise:

What did you talk to your angels about today? Think about it and journal about it.

# November 15

## Dear Archangel Chamuel,

How can you help us in our everyday life?

## Dear Child,

I am the Archangel who can help you find peace in the different relationships you have in your life. You can speak with me or ask for guidance when there is an issue with a relationship. If the relationship is a romantic one, you might want guidance as to whether the relationship is positive for you. You might want guidance on how to solve a disagreement with someone. Please feel free to ask me, Archangel Chamuel, for guidance and assistance. I will help you by my presence and by helping you to see the truth in situations. I can also be there for you as you go through your day with the people who are in your life. Please remember that my main role in helping you is to gently guide you with each issue you have encountered.

## Journal exercise:

Ask for guidance from Archangel Chamuel in the form of a letter to him and then be ready to receive answers back from him in a letter just for you. Think about it and journal about it.

# November 16

*Dear Angels,*

What message do you have for us today?

Today we want to speak about miracles. We want to say that each one of you is a miracle. That every milestone you reach is a miracle and that every vision you manifest is a miracle too. You are a miracle because of your zest for life and your positive outlook. You are a miracle because of who you are and what you have been through in your life.

Don't be afraid to be who you are, because there is just one of you. You make a lot of contributions to the world and people enjoy your uniqueness. You are a co-creator of your life, along with God and your angels. The angels and God guide you. God is the keeper of divine timing and chief organizer for when your manifestations and visions come to fruition. So appreciate the miracle that you are and know that God and the angels are with you at all times.

## *Journal exercise:*

What miracles have happened in your life lately? Think about it and journal about it.

# November 17

Quickly the tears in your eyes were dried off by the sun as the rainbow showed in the sky. The tears that filled your eyes were tears of healing. You could feel the angels with your aura and you knew all was well with you. Love filled your heart and peace and clarity were present. Healing tears are refreshing and there are days when we feel this deep within our core. The angels remind us that we are not alone. They also remind us that we are very much loved by God and the angels.

## Journal exercise:

Have you ever had a time when you felt this love in your heart and felt that all your problems would be taken care of? Think about it and journal about it.

# November 18

*Dear Angels,*

What message do you have for us today?

Sometimes you are too hard on yourself. Give yourself credit for the places in your life where you have grown and flourished. Sometimes the growth is not where you thought it would be. The path you thought you were on might have taken a different direction for a while because there was something you needed to learn. So be patient with this change, try to understand what it is you are supposed to learn and thank all in the Universe for their gentle guidance. Be truly grateful for all of the gifts you have received in recent times. Be open to the opportunities given to you and embrace them fully.

*Journal exercise:*

How have you been hard on yourself lately? How can you be kinder to yourself and feel calmer about manifesting your dreams? Think about it and journal about it.

# November 19

*Dear Angels,*

What message do you have for us today?

When you feel love for yourself or others it brings you to your heart place. Your heart place is always in the same place and you will always find joy and peace there. Let the peace keep you calm and let this calmness give you the clarity that you truly need. We all deserve peace and we all deserve clarity.

## Journal exercise:

There are many different ways in which we can find peace for ourselves. We can do this through music, meditation, walking, jogging, singing or writing. Think about and journal about the ways you find peace for yourself.

# November 20

The angels say that when we are inspired the Universe is speaking to us in a way that we can understand. They say we receive many inspired messages throughout the day, through thoughts that we may not usually have or through something we hear that may help us in our life. There is inspired writing and inspired painting, inspired singing and inspired poetry. Inspiration is the way the Universe helps and reminds us that we are spirits living in a human form. You can also think of being inspired as being *inspirited*.

## Journal exercise:

What and who inspires you in your daily life? Which inspired mediums do you like to use in your life? Think about and journal about it.

# November 21

Release all that hurts you deep within your heart. In its place let the peace and love flow into your heart in a way that is meaningful to you. Let yourself release all that is painful and unbearable. Know that you can heal from this pain that is felt at this time. Let God and the angels take this pain away and let the healing begin.

## Journal exercise:

Giving our pain to the Universe is very healing. What pain would you like to give to the Universe today? Think about it and journal about it.

# November 22

*Dear Angels,*

What message do you have for us today?

Our message to you today is to enjoy life. It is so important to have times when you are having fun. Put away your worries and concerns and give yourself the gift of having fun with people you enjoy. Thanksgiving week is a good time to let yourself have some fun and to enjoy the people who are in your life. Treasure these fun times and be at peace with the clarity of what these fun times mean to you.

*Journal exercise:*

What kind of activities do you like to do when you are being good to yourself? Think about it and journal about it.

# November 23

*Dear Angels,*

What message do you have for us today?

Miracles are gifts from God. They are happy endings for some-thing that otherwise may have ended in sadness. God and the angels work hard each day for these miracles to occur in our lives. Miracles on the Earth plane tell us that God and the angels do exist in our world. They show their love in so many ways, but one of the biggest is through miracles. Be open to the miracles that happen in your life and be forever grateful when they occur. They happen through prayer and meditation and synchronicity. Miracles are the angels' and God's way of saying you are loved and to be at peace for all is well.

*Journal exercise:*

What miracles have happened in your life lately? Think about it and journal about these miracles.

# November 24

*Dear Angels,*

What message do you have for us today?

Our message is to be thankful for the golden peace in your hearts. We thank you for the peace you are instilling on the planet these past months. We thank you for working hard in helping the planet to be more clean and safe. We thank you for your efforts to end starvation around the world. We thank you for your efforts to build homes and schools for those most in need. Thank you for your music. Thank you for the love you show to others. We know it's not easy, but know that you have help and love from all in the Universe.

## Journal exercise:

How do you feel about the angels thanking *you* for the help you have given? Think about it and journal about it.

## November 25

Thank you, angels, for all that you do for us. What words of wisdom do you have for us today?

*Dear Children,*

We want you to know that we love guiding you throughout your day. We love helping you to notice our presence, through the different synchronicities that we present to you. We are pleased when you do notice us and begin to talk to us or talk to others about us. We love seeing the personal growth in each of your lives. We feel your joy when you start looking to the heart place, and then you see the miracles in your life when you live from your heart. Know that we are always with you and we will always help in every way we are able to. Thank you for noticing us as you go through your day.

*Journal exercise:*

If you were able to give a gift to your angels today, what would the gift be? Think about it and journal about it.

# November 26

## Dear Angels,

What message do you have for us today?

Stay in your heart place, which is sacred. Know that you are loved at all times and that you are always acknowledged. We, your angels, love and care for you at all times and want to help you to grow and empower yourselves to become the loving souls that you truly are. Don't be afraid about how this will happen. Just believe in the possibilities and the promises we have made to you. Patience is hard to practice at times, but is something all that are on the Earth plane need to understand and practice. We ask you to enjoy the journey and be at peace with all that occurs in your lifetime.

## Journal exercise:

How do you practice patience on your journey? How have you enjoyed your journey today? Think about it and journal about it.

# November 27

Thank you, dear people, for all you have done in helping others to find the heart place. There is not just one way to find the heart place. There are many different ways to get there. Know that all ways are equal, no one way is better than the other. Let your imagination and your spirit soar, knowing that there are no limits to the creative ways of finding your heart place.

## Journal exercise:

What are some of the creative ways you can find your heart place? Think about it and journal about it.

# November 28

We sometimes say, "Oh, I am not creative and I am not blessed with creative gifts like others have been." This thought can start in childhood and continue well into the autumn years of one's life. The tapes made in childhood play until we can see or understand that they are not the correct tapes to listen to and believe in. The tapes can play even into our seventies and eighties if we don't change them. So change that tape, change that belief that you are not creative! Let your spirit flow and let the creative juices flow, creating in your own way what you feel in your heart place.

## Journal exercise:

What ways do you use your creativity now? What ways would you like to learn about? Think about it and journal about it.

# November 29

When you create artistically, imagine your angels and your Higher Power close to you, helping you to make the final touches to your masterpiece. You can hear their gentle whispers as you present your masterpiece to your "committee" of approval. Then look at what you have created, smile and say, "Wow, I did that?!" This is when you know you have created from the heart place. Imagine your angels dancing with you as you see the true meaning of your masterpiece.

## Journal exercise:

How does it feel to create in the heart place? Think about it and journal about it.

# November 30

How do you know when your heart is singing? It is singing when you see a child laugh, or when you see a field of flowers. Your heart is singing when you watch a romantic movie or hear a favorite song. Your heart is singing when you feel joy and peace and when love is present in your life. How can we not feel the joy in any of these?

## Journal exercise:

What makes your heart sing today? Think about it and journal about it.

# *Living in the Heart place with Your Angels*

# *December Messages*

# December 1

What message do you have for us today?

Let the quiet time be a treasure for you to capture on a daily basis. Take this time for meditation and introspection. We, your angels, ask that you take this time so that you can gather the activities of the day and see where they are heading. We ask you to keep all that is good and to let go of all that is negative. We suggest this because we feel that when you hang on to the negative the brightness of your heart becomes less bright. Let the Universe take away all that is not bright and let go of it so that you may revel in the light.

## Journal exercise:

How can you find quiet time for yourself each morning? Think about it and journal about it.

# December 2

Creativity and intuition go hand and hand together. Creativity is an expression of our higher self through different mediums, such as writing, drawing, painting, sketching, singing, dancing, acting, and doing crafts. The list is endless. We go into a zone that helps us with our creations. It as if we are one with our creation or creative expression. Creativity helps to stretch the mind to places that we did not know before. It helps with self esteem; because we are assured that there are no limits with creative expression of any kind. We can feel the fear and do it anyway.

Fear is one of the reasons we hold back from expressing our creativity. We hear the old tapes that we heard in childhood from family, school and friends. But we can ignore them, because we are in our heart place and there is no room for the old tapes of limitations. Our ability is limitless, so don't be afraid to experiment. Through experimentation we find out what suits us and what we stick with. Yet keeping an open mind and listening to our intuition helps us with new ideas and new ways of learning through creativity, and helps us to be more aware of how intuition works with us. The angels say that inspiration in creativity is paying attention to the nudges we feel inside of us, to create in our own individual way.

## Journal exercise:

What creative medium are you passionate about at this time? How does it help you to know yourself when you are in this zone? Think about it and journal about it.

# December 3

Let the day march to the beat of love that you have in your heart. The beat of this love is the music you feel. Let this music continue to play at all times. Let it comfort you and keep you at peace, for this is your heart song. Your song of love is within you. Let the melody keep you on an even keel throughout the day.

## Journal exercise:

Notice the music playing in your heart place. What does it sound like? Think about it and journal about it.

# December 4

To see yourself as you truly are is a gift from the Universe. When you see your true self, then you know that you are a spiritual being having a human experience. You know that the reality you are seeing is not the true reality of all that you are. You are something higher and more regal than you have ever thought you were. You will see this is in your dreams at night and your day dreams during the day. What are these dreams? Are they an extension of your Higher Self or messages from an angel? Let the truth come out when you are meditating or relaxing. What are you channeling and from whom is it coming? Hearing these messages clearly and seeing yourself as a spiritual being takes time. It doesn't happen overnight. It is something that evolves with your growth and spiritual development.

## Journal exercise:

In what ways do you understand that you are a spiritual being? Think about it and journal about it.

# December 5

What message do you have for us today?

Beauty is all around you, to hold in your heart. Feel the peace in your heart. Feel the calm and serenity there. Be at peace for all is well, and all is taken care of with much love from the Universe.

## Journal exercise:

Go to your heart place and feel the calm and serenity there. What is that like? Think about it and journal about it.

# December 6

*Dear Angels,*

What is your message for us today?

Children, be at peace for all is well. Know that your knowledge is important for you. Be at peace, for you are safe and protected, especially if you are in pain at this time. Ask the questions that may be hard to ask, but whose answers you need to know. Ask the angels to help you with anything that is difficult. They can help you find the answers and can help you to help yourself. Never doubt your questions. Be proactive in what you want to learn about. The Universe wants to help you and show you how to gather your information.

## *Journal exercise:*

What is a difficult question you want an answer for at this time? Ask your angels and see what response you get. Think about it and journal about it.

# December 7

If the choice you make leads to danger ask your Higher Power (God) and your angels to help you back to safety. It may not be the route you want to be on, but it is where you need to be at this time. Thank your angels and God for helping you see the danger that lurked ahead and bringing you to a safer path. Many paths can be difficult, but there is a difference between difficulty and danger. Be grateful that the path you were put back on is the right road, even with its difficult times. Be assured that God and your angels know the right road for you. Patience is called for, and trust is paramount, in this journey called life.

## Journal exercise:

Has there been a time in your life when God and your angels guided you from danger onto the safer road? Think about it and journal about it.

# December 8

*Dear Children,*

Let the ego go by the wayside and let your heart come to the forefront. Let your heart shine brightly with the love of your angels and Higher Power. Create the life that you want to share with all you know. Healing from the hurts of life brings you to a place of peace and love. The peace in your heart can be shared with all. Letting only the good into your heart will protect the uniqueness of who you truly are.

## Journal exercise:

How is your life different when you are coming from your heart place? Think about it and journal about it.

# December 9

"There are many paths to Enlightenment. Be sure to take one that has heart." Author Unknown

The angels say that when we listen to our intuition, we will feel it in our heart. We will feel the positive feeling that lets us know the decision is the right one. The angels say you can't go wrong with this. They also say that our intuition will bring our hearts to a place where we are comfortable and at peace. The heart place is where love is truly felt. The angels say to take some time and go to the heart place and discern the choices that are best for you or for those involved in your decisions. Don't be afraid to ask your angels for some input too. They are with you always. You just need to ask them for assistance and guidance.

## Journal exercise:

What decision do you need to make that you would like help with from the angels? Think about it and journal about it.

# December 10

The angels say that when you look within your heart for answers, they come to you easily. Opening your heart will help you to be inspired with the right answers. Looking to the Universe and to God and your angels, inspiration will come to you immediately. You see, we humans are spiritual beings in a physical body. Our Higher Self will show us the way to the heart. Our angels and the entire Universe give us the guidance we need. They bring positive thoughts and love and peace to our hearts. When we let them do this our hearts are overflowing with love and we know that we are with our angels.

## Journal exercise:

How can you open your heart and hear the messages of your angels and your Higher Self? Think about it and journal about it.

# December 11

Living in the heart place helps you to stay centered in a place that is healing. We know that when healing takes place, the heart becomes softer and your light a little bit brighter. Asking the angels for help with healing can make the process of healing fall into place. Day to day you will see the progress and feel the weight being lifted and the stress falling away like the layers of an onion. Each day is a step closer to healing the issues in your life. Let the process happen and feel your heart become healed.

## Journal exercise:

How have your angels helped you to heal your heart? Think about it and journal about it.

# December 12

We each have our own preferences for what we want in our lives. We need to honor other people's preferences and decisions in their own lives. Accepting that others have their own way of thinking, which is different from ours, will make life a lot easier. The angels feel that when we accept this, there can be harmony between people. Forcing your ideas or beliefs on other people can cause many problems. Understand that everyone has free will, just as you have free will in all that you do. Living in harmony is possible if you understand that we all have free will and our own lessons to learn. Ask your angels for guidance in this and see where they lead you.

## Journal exercise:

How have the angels helped you in understanding that we all have free will? Think about it and journal about it.

# December 13

Living in the present will help you take the next step forward. It will help you focus on the many choices that are before you at this time. Going with the flow, and feeling truly what is in your heart, will help you to know what it is you need to do next. The angels can help you with guidance and with the choices you need to make at this time. When you are in your heart place, a place of wonder and clarity, you will know the right step to take, because there is no resentment or anger there. From this place you can discover what will help you to move on to a place of newness and enlightenment.

## Journal exercise:

How has focusing on the present helped you take a step forward in your life? Think about it and journal about it.

# December 14

## Dear Angels,

What message do you have for us today?

Preparing for the holiday season, as many do during this month, we ask you to take time for yourself. It can be difficult when so much is happening. There are planning, shopping, holiday parties and activities with family and friends. It can all be very exhausting. Many of you feel that you have to be available for everything that is happening. We, your angels, want to remind you that that can be very difficult for many of you. We suggest that you do only what you are able to do during this time. Please don't let yourself become overtaxed. Enjoy the month and make lots of lists to help you with planning all that needs to be done, for you and your family…We also suggest that you do something just for you.

## Journal exercise:

This month what is one thing you can do that is special, just for you? Think about it, journal about it, and do it.

# December 15

We, your angels, help you to deal with fears that trouble you. Sometimes your fears can paralyze you and keep you from moving on in our life. The fear is real and deeply felt. If you ask the angels to show you how to let go of the fear in small steps they will show you how to do this. Sometimes they will send people into your life to help you let go of the fear or to help you with gentle words Once you ask for help notice the subtle changes taking place in how you deal with your fear.

## Journal exercise:

Write a letter to your angels about helping you to overcome a certain fear. Then write a letter replying to your request. Think about it and journal about it.

# December 16

We, your angels and God, want to say to you, "Know that we are with you always, in times of difficultly and in times of peace and forgiveness." Know that when you are able to forgive, you reward yourself with the gift of freedom and release of grudges towards others. You release yourself from the burden of carrying these grudges. When you release and forgive, you feel lighter. You can move on with your life and live the life that you truly would like for yourself. You are not only free to move on, you are free to try new things and to leave the old pain in the past...Living your life to the fullest is what we, your angels and God, want for you.

## Journal exercise:

Who in your life do you need to forgive at this time? Will you ask the angels or God for help, or will you ask both? Think about it and journal about it.

# December 17

What is the way to help others in healing the body, mind and spirit? It is helping them to know that they can be self-healers, through meditation and positive thoughts toward the ailment or emotion that needs to be healed. They can trust the Universe, knowing that they can be healed through self-healing and hands-on and distance healing from others. They can know that the body is self healing, as when a cut heals, and also know that the power of positive thinking helps with healing. People are able to come back from the most horrific body trauma and from disease through imagining themselves as well and completely healed. Everyone has this capability.

The angels remind you to ask them for help with the ailment or emotional pain that is within you. Ask your healing angels to surround you at all times and help you see that healing is taking place. Letting them do the work and being in places that are stress-free, as well as full of joy and laughter, can help the healing process. Know that positive visualization is very powerful for the healing process. Trust is paramount for the healing to happen.

## Journal exercise:

What information have you found about self-healing? Do you believe you can do it? Think about it and journal about it.

# December 18

Angels above, angels below

Sitting quietly, going with the flow.

Whispering sweet nothings especially for me

Thanking them for sharing their glee.

They say they have a message for all who are here

So they may share their wisdom with all who are near.

The angels say that they share with us, that they care

And will never give out information, which is not fair.

Today's message, they want us to know,

Is to let the Universe do the work and go with the flow.

This is not an easy task, any way you throw the ball

They remind us to let them do the work, and you will hear their call.

The angels like to remind you of how happy they are that you trust.

Thanking the angels daily is most certainly a must.

So if you doubt your angels at any given time,

Listen carefully to their words, for all will be fine.

## *Journal exercise:*

See if the angels have a poem for you. Think about it and journal about it.

# December 19

The angels want you to know that you deserve to heal. Healing from the pain of the past will help you to move on in your life and help you keep from experiencing further pain. Sometimes you may think it's the way life is, because it's all you've known. You don't know that you deserve better. Helping yourself to heal will help you to get out of the painful moments. When you are healing, you can ask for guidance from your angels. They can help you to know the best way to heal and the best ways to move on with your life. Archangel Raphael reminds you that he is there for you at all times. Archangel Michael reminds you that he is there in times of trouble and great pain. Don't be afraid to ask these angels for help with the healing of whatever pain you need to heal. When healing the pain, the message to give your angels and yourself is, "No more, I will not continue in this way." Cutting the cords from someone who is part of the pain is a good way to start. You do not forget but you can forgive in a way that helps you to move on to new and more healthy experiences. Everyone has the right to feel that they can heal the pain that they are feeling. Whether it is healing from a long-ago incident, or something that is more recent, the angels ask you to consider the different ways to begin the healing process. Ask for help in this and you will receive guidance from your angels.

## Journal exercise:

Do you have a painful incident that you would like to ask the angels to help you heal? Think about it and journal about it.

# December 20

*Dear Angels,*

What message do you have for us today?

Coming from a place of love, we ask that you listen to what is in your heart. Letting love into the heart place, you can hear the messages of your angels. Hearing their sweet words of encouragement and guidance will help you follow the direction that your heart is giving you. Don't be afraid to listen to the angels, for there will not be harm done. Angels have a direct line of communication to the all-loving source we call God, Allah, Buddha, Yahweh and so on. You see, angels are the loving extension and messengers of this Higher Power. They can encourage you and make the path of whatever direction your life is going a bit easier. They are the light that shows you the way. They also share their light with you as you share yours with all who come to know you. When you share your light, you inspire others to share their light too. God's light is in all places, it is just a matter of choosing to see this light…When living in the heart place, you see this light more easily and you have clarity on your path.

## Journal exercise:

When you are in your heart place, do you find it easier to perceive the light of God and the angels? Think about it and journal about it.

# December 21

*Dear Children,*

When life gets difficult and busy take time to slow down and be at peace for a few minutes. Sit down and take a minute to breathe and take inventory of where you are going and what you are doing. If your day is wildly busy, can certain things be done tomorrow so that you are able to have some free time for yourself or with family or friends? Try to pace yourself so you don't get overworked. Take some time to just sit and relax. Make your plans for tomorrow and the next day and know that life's little chores don't have to all be done today.

## Journal exercise:

Make a list of the errands that need to done the next few days. Ask your angels for guidance. Think about it and journal about it.

# December 22

We, your angels, ask you to think about the events of the past year and take inventory of what the year was like. Check in and see what you feel were the highpoints of your year. Were your goals for this year achieved? What goals fell by the wayside? Then think about next year and what you would like to accomplish next. Make lists and figure out what is important for your next year. We just want you to know that taking stock of the past year and having some goals for the next year is a good way to see how far you have come in the past year and where you can grow further.

## Journal exercise:

What goals do you have for the next year? Think about it and journal about it.

# December 23

We, your angels, want to remind you of the different holiday traditions that are being celebrated around the world this month. We ask you to remain open to all celebrations and to take part in many of these celebrations, if an opportunity comes to you to do so. The experience can be very enlightening when you have an open mind. It can be interesting to see the types of prayers used and what the focus is of different beliefs. It can be fun to taste new foods offered at these events. Try inviting friends or family with different beliefs to your house to share their celebrations. Being open to different traditions during this month will surely be enriching for all. We wish you an enjoyable holiday season.


## Journal exercise:

Have you ever taken part in observing a holiday tradition different from your own? Think about it and journal about it.

# December 24

When you glow from the inside and on the outside you know that you are in your heart place. You know because of how you feel. You will also know because people will tell you so. There is a feeling of complete joy and satisfaction with who you are. The angels bring you much joy but you are the one who allows the joy in. Don't forget to count your blessings for all that you are and that you will be. There is so much satisfaction when feeling so at peace and joyful. When this joy is there, no one can make you feel bad, ever.


## Journal exercise:

Have you ever felt like you were glowing with peace and joy? Think about it and journal about it.

# December 25

In the spirit of the season we thank our angels and Higher Power for the blessings given to us. We thank the Universe for the love and guidance that we receive. The promise of love and peace are relevant for this day. The angels have a message for all who are here now, Children, we thank you for your love and support. We thank you for the progress made in helping to enlighten others about the gifts the Universe has given. This is the season for love and for clarity about your place in the world. Know that you matter and that you have been very helpful in enlightening others.

## Journal exercise:

What blessings are you grateful for? Think about it and journal about it.

# December 26

Listen to your heart today. What is it telling you? How do you feel about this? Can you do something to improve the situation? Is there something you need to do or is there someone you need to call or write to? How can the feeling of bliss be put back into your day? Maybe the bliss is already there. Maybe you need to go within some more. Ask the angels and your guides for help if you need assistance. Your heart will tell you what it is you need. Take away the sad feeling if you are feeling blue, or enjoy the feeling of joy that is in your heart at this time. You can ask your angels to show you the way and they will help you. Asking yourself some of these questions daily can help you to be grounded and centered in your heart. It is important to be aware of all your feelings and not dismiss them as inconsequential. You aren't alone, no matter what. Try doing some meditation or completing the task that is nagging at you.

Procrastination shows up in many different ways. The angels say that when procrastination is dealt with, joy is felt, for you have no longer put off your task. Then you can relax and feel what it's like to have completed the issue or task that needed to be finished.

## Journal exercise:

What task have you been putting off? How can the angels help you? Think about it and journal about it.

# December 27

When listening to the angels sing, you hear their wonderful songs of joy and love for you. We, your angels, ask you to feel deep within your heart the tune so clear. Listening to the pledge of love and peace, you know your angels are speaking clearly. They sing of their clear vision and dreams for you…They are the same dreams that you have for yourself. The angels are with you all through the day, and they show you this in many, many ways. The feather you find in the grass today is from them to let you know they are there for you. The songs that catch your attention and share a message or the book that may fall off the shelf let you know that they are there. They will never leave you, but if you were to ask them to do so, then your wish would be granted. The angels can help you to let go of your worries and troubles. You just have to ask for help with this and they will be there for you immediately. Self doubt will wash away, as the healing tears of your heart become a rainbow of joy.


## Journal exercise:

What is your heart telling you today? Think about it and journal about it.

# December 28

So many today think that the angels look down upon them and just view the goings-on of their lives. The angels want you to know that they are with you, in front of you, behind you, next to you, all around you. Sometimes you will feel them as a soft touch or a gentle breeze. This will tell you they are near. Archangel Michael wants you to know that he is very close, waiting for you to speak to him about something that is important to you. He is always ready to help when you ask. Archangel Raphael helps with personal healing and with channeling healing to others through reiki or hands-on or distance healing. He is always ready to help. Gabriel has special messages for you and he is ready to convey them to you. The other angels are with you, too.

Imagine a group of angels and your guides gathered behind you, ready to help when called upon. Look for the synchronicities that happen throughout the day. These are messages that come from God and your angels. The angels delight in whispering these messages to you. Enjoy all that you receive, for you too are a child of God.

## Journal exercise:

Which angel are you speaking with today? Think about it and journal about it.

# December 29

Angels and moonbeams, butterflies and rainbows, are all symbols that can be given to you when speaking with the angels. These symbols help you to understand their messages. They can be given in a different way to each person receiving a message. The angels say, "We take into consideration what a certain symbol means for you. As you know, the symbols convey a positive message to the person receiving them. We feel a symbol that is positive will help you understand more deeply what the message means." There are so many songs about angels, moonbeams, butterflies and rainbows, there are stories and meditations, books and movies about our angels and the symbols that are associated with them. When you receive symbols and messages pay attention to them and see if you are able to understand why you are receiving this message.

## Journal exercise:

The symbols you receive when getting a message are specific to you. What are some of the symbols you've received? Think about it and journal about it.

# December 30

The angels want you to know they also have a sense of humor. Many of their messages are given with a sense of humor because laughter and joy are so good for you. When using your sense of humor, you feel much lighter and you may even begin to smile or laugh out loud. The angels laugh with you. It clears your mood and you feel understood, even if it is a bit silly at times. They ask you to not be afraid to let the humor come through. They love to laugh and to laugh with you. May your angels on the moonbeams be with you in the form of butterflies as they fly through the rainbow today. Angel blessings to all.

## Journal exercise:

In what ways have the angels shown you their humor recently? Think about it and journal about it.

# December 31

A new year is upon you and life is so good. You have so many plans and dreams that you want to have happen. There are people to meet, places to go, dreams to be imagined, so go with the flow. The New Year will begin in a few hours you know, then ring in the year and feel all the joy. You may be with friends and with family, speaking of your plans. The advice we, your angels, give to you at this time is to prioritize and plan bit by bit. Have fun as you do this and get the important things out of the way. Then know in your heart as you smile today, that angels are truly with you in so many ways.

## Journal exercise:

What plans do you have for the New Year? Think about it and journal about it.

# Final Message from the Angels

When I finished all 366 messages from my angels I asked them if they had a final message for all of us.

## Dear Angels,

What is your final message to us, concerning this book?

## Dear Children,

We would like to say that completing this book is a joyous moment for us as we see you reading this book. We carefully directed the way in which the messages were written. The translations of these messages are truly wonderful. Two years is a long time to be channeling messages from us. It shows dedication and a determination of completing a task that was asked of Peg from her angels.

In relaying these messages to Peg, we hope that they will help anyone who is interested in getting to know us, your Angels. There all types of exercises in this book, which will help you to do this. As you read the messages each day notice how the exercise helps you to get just a bit closer to your angels and communicate with us more easily. We wish you many wonderful days on your life's path. We look forward to hearing from you as you journal each day. This book is about discovery and who your angels are. It is about asking for conscious guidance from us, your angels, and learning who you are too.

We thank you all who have read this book.

Love, the Angels

# About Peg Jones

Peg Jones, ALC is an Angelic Life Coach and is also an international Teacher of classes about the angels and how we can connect with the angels through journaling and meditation Her two main classes are Angels 101 and Writing with the Angels. Peg also teaches a 12 week Angel Communication class. Peg has written for several e-zines around the net and has a monthly column on Pencil Stubs e-zine, called Angel Whispers. She offers angel intuitive messages to those who have questions about their personal issues and also offers individual messages from their angels. Peg is also a Reiki 2 practitioner and a practitioner of the Akashic Records. Pegs website is http://pegsangelicalwhispers.com.

## Angelical Whispers

*Let your angels put your priorities in order.*

# Some testimonials about Peg's channeled messages from the Angels:

*"Peg's angelical messages speak to my heart. She is an amazing woman with gifts that inspire and uplift. The angels speak to us through her, with insightful and transformational messages that, if you let them, can change your life."* T.J. Phillips 3/09/03

*"Thank you Peg for the wonderfully inspiring messages, keep them coming please! Many Blessings"* Julia Haynes, Yorkshire, England

*"The messages from the Angels as received and posted by Peg Jones in Face Book have been a source of daily inspiration to me. Life isn't always simple but I can face things with a more positive attitude because of these messages. Everyone is not able to communicate effectively with heavenly sources but apparently there is a blessed flow from the Angels into Peg's heart. That blessing comes through her writing into our own heart. Thank you, Peg Jones."* Mary E. Adair, Texas

*"Peg Wolf-Jones consistently gave accurate and comforting messages for me that I have found to be both useful and comforting."* Mary A. Kisor

*"I met Peg many years ago, just as she was beginning to walk her spiritual path. It has been a pleasure and a privilege to watch her amazing journey since then.*

*Over the years I have watched Peg work in Spiritual Healing where she has always shown a deep understanding of people's needs in a sensitive and respectful way.*

*Peg is also an Angelic Life Coach and I have received wonderful messages from the Angels directed through her. She also gives daily messages from the Angels which give great support and inspiration to many people."*
*Barbara MacFarlane*

"I have had the gift of knowing Peg for several years now. On many occasions when felt "stuck" upon my own path-or perhaps unsure of which path to take, Peg has been able to share with me, though her Angel work-precise, insightful, compassionate guidance I found to be "spot on" for where I was, and what I needed to hear. Through her communications, you feel directly, gently guided by Angelic realms and very loved. Peg's personal compassionate way of listening is a very warm and welcoming opening to the loving messages she brings." Nancy Park, Medium

"Peg shares inspiring messages from the beloved angels that are so timely! My heart is touched! Always a message that one needs to know....that we are blessed, that we are protected and most important, we are never alone on our journey. Every message is an inspiration! I am grateful.. No doubt the inspiration is God sent." Carol Odehnal Howitt

"I have known Peg Wolf for ten years. Peg and her husband are exemplary Christians who truly live their faith. Peg's love of the Lord and gift of Communication with Spirit and angels has been with her since young childhood realized the presence of her Guardian Angel. Peg has spent time doing beautiful caring works and prayerful time listening to the Lord's promptings in her life and the guidance of the angels.

I have enjoyed and been inspired by her angel messages for several years. She has now composed a book from her personal journals that will give everyone who desires, a closer relationship with the Lord and guidance of their angels by experiencing the messages that she has received and the ability to look to the angels on their own for comfort and awareness. Thank you, Peg for sharing the treasures of the angels." Gerri

Peg has been such a comfort and joy to talk to and so this testimonial for her. She has given me such great messages from the ANGELS that no one else ever has and has guided me in the right

389

direction. I trust her with her words and have really given me great in-site with-in my own life. Her herself is an ANGEL in disguise. I have gotten to love Peg. May God bless her and her works with the Angels and in helping just so many others around the country." Becky Tilton

"It seemed every day, I needed to hear a message, Peg would post her lovely message to us from the angels! And even though the message was always meant for everyone, I felt like they were just talking to me every time! I cannot thank Peg enough for insightful and beautiful messages from the angels. Thank you Peg, you are a gift and blessing to us all."
Love, Light and Peace,
Janey

20450503R00216

Made in the USA
Charleston, SC
11 July 2013